ADDING IT UP

Math for Your Cosmetology Career

Kathi A. Dunlap

DELMAR PUBLISHERS INC.®

Cover design by Anne Pompeo

Milady Staff:
      Sponsoring Editor: Anne Lowenthal
      Production Manager: John Mickelbank
Delmar Staff:
      Project Editor: Carol Micheli
      Project Coordinator: Wendy Troeger

Printed in the United States of America
published simultaneously in Canada
by Nelson Canada,
a division of The Thomson Corporation

10 9 8 7 6 5 4 3 2 1

Library of Congress Cataloging in Publication Data

Dunlap, Kathi A.
   Adding it up : math for your cosmetology career / Kathi A. Dunlap.
     p. cm.
   ISBN (invalid) 0-562-53063-3
   1. Beauty culture—Mathematics. 2. Beauty shops—Management—
Mathematics. I. Title.
TT958.D86   1992
646.7'2'01513—dc20
                        91-28025
                          CIP

Contents

Introduction

ADDING IT UP Math for Your Cosmetology Career is designed to help develop the math skills necessary to work in the field of cosmetology. The chapters are written in a clear, concise manner with easy-to-follow examples. Each chapter offers both numerical problems to develop the skills presented and word problems to apply those skills to the field of cosmetology. *ADDING IT UP Math for Your Cosmetology Career* is appropriate for use in the vocational/technical area of cosmetology. It can be used as the main text in a cosmetology math class or as a supplemental cosmetology curriculum text.

The book begins with coverage of basic mathematic operations such as place values, whole number operations, decimal operations, fractions, and percents (Chapters 1–5). Although these skills are a review for many students, they are presented thoroughly enough to provide a clear understanding of the concepts.

The next section (Chapters 6–9) presents the math concepts necessary to accomplish some of the hands-on skills of cosmetology. Ratios and proportions are introduced (for mixing solutions) as well as measurement and the geometry of angles. These chapters provide a solid mathematical base to assist the students in their laboratory skills.

Chapters 10–15 cover various aspects related to shop ownership and personal finance. Time management, money management, and business mathematics are presented. Again, word problems are presented throughout to help the student to apply what they are learning.

This text can be used in sequence to provide a logical, sound mathematic curriculum for a cosmetology student. However, each chapter stands by itself so that topics can be rearranged and adapted to the cosmetology curriculum.

To the Student

When you watch a cosmetologist work, it appears that they are using only their hands to perform their duties. A look behind the scenes, however, shows that there is much more to it. Along with the "hands-on" skills, there are many other factors involved with being a good cosmetologist. One of these skills is mathematics.

At what angle do you roll a curl? How much hair should you cut off? How do you make sanitization solutions for your implements? When should you schedule your appointments? How do you order supplies for your shop? How much money will you make? What about payroll if you have employees?

This book will emphasize the math skills needed to perform your cosmetology skills. The text provides opportunity to review basic math skills and it also offers many new concepts, unique to the cosmetology field. A major emphasis is placed on business and personal finance. Since many cosmetologists own their own business (or manage a business), a thorough understanding of business skills is necessary.

Even though math is not an *obvious* part of your career, it is a very important part. It provides the background for much of what you do with your hands.

Chapter 1

Place Values

Place Values

The place values in our number system are:

1,000,000	100,000	10,000	1,000	100	10	units	.	10th	100th	1000th	10,000th	100,000th	1,000,000th

Knowing these place values is important in many mathematical operations such as rounding numbers, comparing numbers, reading numbers, or lining up columns to add. It is also important when writing out numbers as words for checks or receipts.

The places to the right of the decimal all end in "th" and are **part** of a whole number. The places to the left of the decimal all indicate multiples of a whole number. When a number does not have a decimal in it, assume that the decimal is at the right. For example, 74 is understood to mean 7 tens and 4 units and the decimal belongs to the right (74.).

Example 1: Determine what place value the underlined digit holds in 526.78<u>3</u>5

Since the underlined digit is in the third place right of the decimal it is in the thousandths place.

Example 2: Determine what place value the underlined digit holds in .0035<u>3</u>31

Since the underlined digit is in the fifth place right of the decimal, it is in the hundred-thousandths place.

Example 3: Determine what place value the underlined digit holds in 4,561,<u>6</u>35.26

Since the underlined digit is in the third place left of the decimal, it is in the hundreds place.

Example 4: Determine what place value the underlined digit holds in 4,57<u>3</u>,671

When a number does not have a decimal point written, the point is assumed to be at the right of the number. This number could be rewritten as 4,57<u>3</u>,671. with a decimal point. Since the underlined digit is in the fourth place left of the decimal, it is in the thousands place.

Problems State the place value of the underlined number.

1) 724.<u>8</u> _____

2) 1<u>0</u>,429 _____

3) 4.3<u>6</u>71 _____

4) <u>9</u>.83 _____

5) <u>2</u>14.53 _____

6) <u>1</u>00,000.1 _____

7) <u>3</u>6495 _____

8) 8<u>6</u> _____

9) 4.6<u>7</u>5 _____

10) 82.00<u>1</u> _____

11) 46.898<u>9</u> _____

12) 46,<u>8</u>92 _____

13) 8.0<u>0</u>1 _____

14) 47.7<u>9</u>6 _____

15) <u>5</u>21 _____

16) 842<u>6</u>2 _____

17) <u>3</u>9.417 _____

18) 8,<u>6</u>13,218.4 _____

19) 1,3<u>7</u>6,582 _____

20) 34<u>2</u>9.63 _____

Indicate which of the digits (0–9) are in the specified place value in this number: 9,876,543.210

Example: Which digit is in the tenths place? The tenths place is just to the right of the decimal. Therefore, the two is in the tenths place.

21) tenths	_____	26) hundreds	_____
22) tens	_____	27) 10,000s	_____
23) units	_____	28) 1000s	_____
24) millions	_____	29) 100,000s	_____
25) 1000ths	_____	30) 100ths	_____

Comparing Numbers

Comparing numbers is necessary in preparing cleaning solutions or making change. It is also useful in many office skills, such as numerical filing, ordering supplies, figuring parts of a payroll, and so on.

To compare numbers, first line up the decimal points. This is a process of putting certain place values of one number above the same place value of the other number or numbers.

117.68   The units (for example) are on top of each other.
111.452

Then, beginning from left to right, compare like place values. The digits in the hundreds place in both numbers are the same. The digits in the tens place in both numbers are the same. The units place is where the first difference occurs. Since the 1 in 111.452 is smaller than the 7 in 117.68, 111.452 is the smaller number.

Sometimes the numbers you are comparing do not have the same number of place values. When this occurs, the number which holds the highest place value is the largest. For example,

11768.2   holds the ten thousands place
1176.82   holds the thousands place

Therefore 11768.2 is larger than 1176.82 because the ten thousands place is larger than the thousands place.

This could also be determined by the original method if you realize that any place value that is "empty"—no digit in that place value—has a value of zero. So,

11768.2   has a one in the ten thousands place
01176.82   has a zero in the ten thousands place

11768.2 is determined to be larger than 1176.82 using this method as well, since one is larger than zero.

Example 1: Which is larger: 0.70 ?
                            0.713

Looking from left to right, the first digits that are different are in the hundredths place. Since 1 is larger than nothing at all, 0.713 is larger.

Example 2: Which is larger: 2960.5 ?
                                     2956.83

Looking from left to right, the first digits that are different are in the tens place. Since 6 is larger than five, 2960.5 is larger than 2956.83.

Example 3: Which is larger: .1   ?
                                     .0602

Looking from left to right, the zero and one in the tenths place are different. Since 1 is larger than zero, .1 is larger than .0602.

Example 4: Which is larger: 17?
                                     .135

In this case, the two numbers do not share any of the same place values. You can determine which number is larger if you recognize that 17 is a whole number (17 complete units) and .135 is only part of a whole number (part of one unit). Seventeen complete units is larger than just a part of one unit. Another method of determining which number is larger involves filling in some place values with zeros for comparison.

$$\underline{1}7$$
$$\underline{0}0.135$$

Since the digit one that holds the tens place in 17 is larger than zero, 17 is larger than .135.

Problems   Line up the place values before comparing numbers.

A. Circle the larger of the two numbers.

1) 4.786	11) 3	21) 151.1
4.7	15	111
2) 5.39	12) 89	22) 36.8
53	90	36.799
3) 6.002	13) 2173	23) 2577
6.2	220.3	527
4) 40,000	14) 5.001	24) 38.96
4962	5.0	39.01
5) 73.6	15) 6159	25) 2.65
700	6200	2.069
6) 9.209	16) 8.4	26) 51
9.21	9.1	50.8
7) 468	17) 26.3	27) 776
486	.795	7676
8) 6.3	18) 100	28) 98
6.03	100.06	907.9
9) 49288	19) 53	29) 8010
49300	52.869	8100
10) 8.21	20) 416	30) 453.2
8.4	42.9	2545

4   PLACE VALUES

B. Circle the number that is not equal to the others.

31) 8.010	32) 53.6	33) 1000.2	34) 57.606	35) .001
8.100	53.60	1000.20	57.6060	.0010
8.01	53.06	1002.0	57.60600	.1010
8.01000		1000.200	57.60660	0.001

Rounding Numbers

To round numbers to a certain place value, it is first necessary to determine where that place value is. Then you can use the number directly to the right of that place value to decide whether or not to round the original place value. If the right digit is 5 or larger, round up the original digit to the next largest number. If it is less than 5, leave the original digit alone.

When you are rounding to a certain place value, your final answer will have no digits of value to the right of that place value. The only digit which should remain to the right is zero.

Example 1:   Round 5.9267 to the 100th place.

1) Where is the 100th place? 5.9267
2) Use digit to the right to decide. 5.9267
3) Since 6 is in the "5 or larger" category, round the 2 up. (Change the remaining digits to zeros— or leave them off.)
4) Solution is: 5.93

Example 2:   Round 531.89 to the 100s place.

1) Where is the 100s place? 531.89
2) Use the digit to the right to decide. 531.89
3) Since 3 is in the "less than 5" category, leave the 5 alone. Change remaining digits to zeros.
4) Solution is: 500.00 or 500 (Since these are equivalent numbers, either solution is permissible.)

Example 3:   Round 57.38 to the nearest unit.

1) Where is the units place? 57.38
2) Use the digit to the right to decide. 57.38
3) Round up or leave alone? Leave alone.
4) Solution is: 57.00 or 57

Problems   Round the following numbers to the specified place value.

A.   Round to the nearest 1000.

1) 57,263 ____	4) 3,965 ____	7) 876,521 ____
2) 981 ____	5) 2175 ____	8) 430,020 ____
3) 3176.5 ____	6) 4616.99 ____	9) 27,647,531 ____

B.   Round to the nearest 100.

1) 57,263 ____	4) 3,965 ____	7) 876,521 ____
2) 981 ____	5) 2175 ____	8) 430,020 ____
3) 3176.5 ____	6) 4616.99 ____	9) 27,647,531 ____

C.   Round to the nearest 10.

1) 57,263 ____	4) 3,965 ____	7) 876,521 ____
2) 981 ____	5) 2175 ____	8) 430,020 ____
3) 3176.5 ____	6) 4616.99 ____	9) 27,647,531 ____

D.   Round to the nearest unit.

1) 4.77653 _____   4) 81.4753 _____   7) 4.00605 _____
2) 7.4939 _____   5) 213.6168 _____ 8) 2.7893 _____
3) 51.673 _____   6) 11.1111 _____   9) 5.1515 _____

E.   Round to the nearest 10th.

1) 4.77653 _____   4) 81.4753 _____   7) 4.00605 _____
2) 7.4939 _____   5) 213.6168 _____ 8) 2.7893 _____
3) 51.673 _____   6) 11.1111 _____   9) 5.1515 _____

F.   Round to the nearest 100th.

1) 4.77653 _____   4) 81.4753 _____   7) 4.00605 _____
2) 7.4939 _____   5) 213.6168 _____ 8) 2.7893 _____
3) 51.673 _____   6) 11.1111 _____   9) 5.1515 _____

G.   Round to the nearest 1000th.

1) 4.77653 _____   4) 81.4753 _____   7) 4.00605 _____
2) 7.4939 _____   5) 213.6168 _____ 8) 2.7893 _____
3) 51.673 _____   6) 11.1111 _____   9) 5.1515 _____

H.   Round to the appropriate place value.

10th   units   hundreds
1) 4.796 _____   4) 89.65 _____   7) 2119.4 _____
2) 34.87 _____   5) 4.332 _____   8) 806.5 _____
3) 2.115 _____   6) 8.5 _____   9) 21,768 _____

1000ths   tens   100ths
10) 4.11654 _____   13) 147.616 _____   16) 5.776 _____
11) 3.7547 _____   14) 81.4 _____   17) 8.9999 _____
12) .00129 _____   15) 363.83 _____   18) 236.417 _____

Reading and Writing Numbers as Words

To read numbers out loud correctly, it is helpful to separate the number into parts. It is also necessary to know the place values learned in the previous section.

Example 1:   Read 6027498.1

1) First, separate the left side into the traditional units by commas (every three digits from the decimal). 6027498.1 becomes 6,027,498.1

2) Next, read each section separately, stating the digits and the place value of the last digit. (Hundreds are usually stated whenever number are in groups of three, as seen in this example):

3)   Next   *SAY...*

	digit	place value
6,	6	million
027,	27	thousand
498	498	(omit saying "units" and say "and" instead)
.1	1	tenth

OR 6 million, 27 thousand, 4 hundred 98 and 1 tenth

Thus, the word "and" separates the whole number (left side) from the part of a whole number (right side). Do not say "and" if there is nothing on the right side.

Example 2:   Read 4965.821

1) 4965.821 becomes 4,965.821
2) Next   *SAY...*

4,	4	thousand
965	965	"and"
.821	821	thousandths

     OR 4 thousand, 9 hundred 65 and 8 hundred 21 thousandths

Example 3:   Read .0046783

1) Nothing on the left side to separate with commas. However, while it is not traditional to separate the right side of the decimal into groups of three with commas, it <u>is</u> helpful to the process of reading and writing numbers as words. Thus, .0046783 will become .0,046,783 (separating into groups of three from the right, not from the decimal).
2) Next   *SAY...*

                   .0,046,783   46,783 ten-millionths

     OR 46 thousand, 7 hundred 83 ten-millionths

Example 4:   Read 25689.004201

1) 25689.004201 becomes 25,689.004201
2) Next   *SAY...*

25,	25	thousand
689	689	"and"
.004201	4,201	millionths

     OR 25 thousand, 6 hundred 89, and 4 thousand 2 hundred and 1 millionths

Problems

A.   Read the following numbers orally.

1) 4296.81	6) 475.31	11) 53274.83
2) 216593	7) 81267.5832	12) 4.76
3) 74.659	8) 772.568	13) 1.005
4) 9.8	9) 27.0003	14) .45
5) 3	10) 270.03	15) .0045

B.   Write these numbers as shown in the examples.

16) 462.373 _____	21) 37.97 _____	26) 18.337 _____
17) 17344.47_____	22) 163.66 _____	27) 28587 _____
18) 274.482 _____	23) 882.22 _____	28) 1563.333 _____
19) 1694869 _____	24) 7390 _____	29) 16.33685 _____
20) .000306 _____	25) 23.6375 _____	30) 2685.9 _____

Chapter 2

Whole Number Operations

Mathematics is an important skill in cosmetology, particularly if you choose to operate your own shop. Even the most basic skills of cosmetology require a knowledge of measurement, awareness of angles, and accuracy in handling money. Being competent in addition, subtraction, multiplication, and division is the basis for accuracy in all other mathematical operations.

Addition

To add whole numbers, it is important to line up the numbers according to place values. Neatness in lining up the columns will insure an accurate total.

$$\begin{array}{r} 2 \\ 108 \\ 13 \\ 17 \\ 22 \\ \underline{7} \\ 167 \end{array}$$

- Add the ones column.
  $$8 + 3 + 7 + 2 + 7 = 27$$
- Write down the 7 and carry the 2 over to the tens column.
- Add the tens column.
  $$2 + 1 + 1 + 2 = 6$$
- Write down the 6 and carry nothing.
- Add the hundreds column, write down, carry if possible.
- Continue until all columns are totalled.

Your addition can be greatly simplified by grouping numbers as you add. Let's look at the ones column again.

$$\begin{array}{r} 108 \\ 13 \\ 17 \\ 22 \\ \underline{7} \\ 167 \end{array}$$

$8 + 2 = 10$
$3 + 7 = 10$
$\underline{7}$
27

- Add any numbers together which together equal ten.
- Then add all remaining numbers in.
  (Solution: 27)

Numbers which add together to equal ten are called *complementary*. These include:

$$1 + 9$$
$$2 + 8$$
$$3 + 7$$
$$4 + 6$$
$$5 + 5$$

When you are adding, look for pairs like this to simplify your work.

Problems   Solve the following problems by lining up the numbers to be added in a vertical column then completing the addition.

1) $2 + 6 + 5 + 9 + 1 + 8 =$ _____

2) $1 + 3 + 4 + 7 + 9 + 6 + 4 =$ _____

3) $8 + 3 + 9 + 7 + 2 =$ _____

4) $6 + 3 + 2 + 8 + 4 =$ _____

5) $14 + 26 + 3 =$ _____

6) $18 + 19 + 22 + 6 =$ _____

7) $6 + 15 + 34 + 8 + 25 =$ _____

8) $4 + 7 + 18 + 6 + 33 =$ _____

9) $3 + 9 + 11 + 27 + 4 =$ _____

10) $8 + 6 + 9 + 3 + 4 + 7 =$ _____

11)
```
  4678
+  481
```

12)
```
  36,158
+  2,488
```

13)
```
  4,846
+   333
```

14)
```
  864
  821
  916
+ 799
```

15)
```
  413
  216
  744
+ 316
```

16)
```
  93
  81
  67
+ 74
```

17)
```
  81
  12
  17
+ 93
```

18)
```
  3,461
    829
    913
+   875
```

19)
```
  63,996
  17,963
+  8,414
```

20)
```
  189,641
+ 328,479
```

21) Janice is required to take inventory at Hudson's Salon every month. She counts the supplies in the dispensary and adds them to find a total inventory. Total the following:

Permanent Waves:
```
    127
     63
    219
    151
+    18
```

Boxes of cotton neck wrap:
```
   8
   3
   2
   4
+ 11
```

Plastic gloves:
```
    586
    211
    394
     88
+  115
```

Hair color solution:
```
   381
   218
   157
   108
+  93
```

22) Janice also has to take inventory of the reception desk and filing area. Total the following:

File Folders:
```
red        81
blue       68
green      52
yellow  + 705
```

Labels:
```
     69
    488
    206
     11
     44
+  817
```

Forms:
```
sales slips          606
customer profiles     81
daily cash reports  + 204
```

23) Sally Ramirez works for Odessey Hair Center in the Bridgemon Mall. She is required to total the number of customers she services every week as well as the hours worked. Complete her report form below.

	customers	hours
Monday	15	6
Tuesday	20	8
Wednesday	9	4
Friday	19	8
Saturday	15	6

24) David is a student at Cosmetology Academy. He must keep an accurate account of hours completed in each of several areas to report to his state board of cosmetology. The form is completed by adding the total for each week in the areas of theory, practice, and clinic. Then, the cumulative total is also found in each area. (You will be adding each column—up and down—and writing the answer at the bottom.)

DATE	LECTURE & THEORY	HR	DEMONSTRATION	HR	PRACTICE	HR	CLINIC	HR
10/7	haircutting	2	haircutting	1	haircutting	1		
	shampoo	1	shampoo	1	shampoo	2		
	scalp care	1			hairstyling	3		
	———		———					
	=							

FIGURE 2-1 Whole number addition on time sheet

25) BONUS: Find the digits that A and B represent.

$$\begin{array}{r} 1,A65,328 \\ +\ \ 476,83A \\ \hline B,44B,167 \end{array}$$

A = _____

B = _____

Subtraction

To subtract whole numbers, it is important to line up the numbers according to place values. Neatness in lining up the columns is essential.

Example 1: Subtract 27 from 139.

1. Begin by placing the number from which you are subtracting on top and place the other number underneath, lining up the units places.

$$\begin{array}{r} 139 \\ -\ 27 \end{array}$$

2. Next, subtract each place value in the bottom number from the appropriate place value above it.

139	units:	$9 - 7 = 2$
− 27	tens:	$3 - 2 = 1$
112	hundreds:	$1 - 0 = 1$

Example 2:   Subtract 63 from 147.

1. Write the problem vertically, the number you are subtracting from on top of the other number.

$$147$$
$$- 63$$

2. Next, subtract each place value in the bottom number from the appropriate place value above it.

147	units:	$7 - 3 = 4$
− 63	tens:	$4 - 6 =$ cannot be done
4		

3. When subtraction cannot be done, you must borrow from the next column to the left. You will be taking one from the hundreds column and renaming it as 10 additional tens to be used for subtraction in the tens place. Now instead of having 4 tens, you have fourteen tens.

147	units:	$7 - 3 = 4$
− 63	tens:	$14 - 6 = 8$
84	hundreds:	there are no hundreds to subtract because you borrowed the only hundred that you had

Sometimes you must borrow from more than one column. Let's look at example 3:

Example 3:   Subtract 97 from 400.

1. Line up the numbers vertically.

$$400$$
$$- 97$$

2. Next, subtract each place value in the bottom number from the appropriate place value above it.

400	units:	$0 - 7 =$ cannot be done
− 97		

Right away, we face the problem of not being able to subtract as the problem is written. It must be rewritten with the appropriate borrowing so that the problem can be completed.

When we try to borrow a ten to bring over to the units as ten units, we find a zero. We must first borrow from the hundreds place to have some tens from which to borrow.

Thus, the 4 hundreds will become three hundreds and the hundred that was borrowed will be renamed as 10 tens.

$$\overset{3\ 10}{4\cancel{0}\cancel{0}}$$
$$- 97$$

We now have some tens from which we can borrow for the units place. We will borrow one of those tens and rename it as 10 units. This leaves us with 3 hundreds, 9 tens and 10 units.

$\overset{3\ 9\ 10}{4\cancel{0}\cancel{0}}$	units:	$10 - 7 = 3$
− 97	tens:	$9 - 9 = 0$
303	hundreds:	$3 - 0 = 0$

Problems   Line up all problems vertically before subtracting.

1) $14 - 8 =$ _____

2) $27 - 19 =$ _____

3) $109 - 46 =$ _____

4) $67 - 23 =$ _____

5) $89 - 21 =$ _____

6) $115 - 47 =$ _____

7) $41 - 9 =$ _____

8) $53 - 36 =$ _____

9) $101 - 74 =$ _____

10) $18 - 6 =$ _____

11) 721
   − 46
	12) 48,610
	   − 396
		13) 3,917
		   − 86
			14) 1,964
			   − 128
				15) 468
				   − 27

16) 3,939
   − 984
	17) 682
	   − 96
		18) 8,416
		   − 767
			19) 409
			   − 89
				20) 1,047
				   − 953

21) a. Janice uses the inventory she takes every month to figure out how many supplies have been used. If she started with 578 permanent waves and is left with 167, how many were used?   _____

   b. If she started with 28 boxes of cotton and is left with 19, how many were used?   _____

   c. If she started with 1,394 pairs of plastic gloves and is left with 995, how many were used?   _____

   d. If she started with 957 appointment cards and is left with 525, how many were used?   _____

22) a. Janice is required to keep a certain amount of all reception area supplies in stock. If she must keep 1,000 file folders on hand and her inventory shows 906, how many more should she order?   _____

   b. If she must keep 2,000 labels on hand and her inventory shows 1,635, how many more should she order?   _____

   c. If she must keep 750 of each of the following forms on hand, how many more of each should she order?   _____

Forms:	sales slips	606
	customer profiles	81
	daily cash reports	204

23) Chris is a sales representative for Highland Lakes Beauty Supply. She is demonstrating some samples of new products to a local beauty shop and they decide to order some of the new products. They order 125 NEW DAY permanent wave kits, 55 OPULESSENCE tint kits, and 10 boxes of cotton. She wants to give them the new products right away, but she did not bring enough with her. How many more of each item will she need to bring to complete their order if she gives them:

   a. 97 permanent wave kits?   _____

   b. 39 tint kits?   _____

   c. 10 boxes of cotton?   _____

24) Beth works as an image consultant. She has been hired by the Boutwell Company to give the executives an analysis of their image and to make recommendations. She has been given a list of all executives and the department they work in. There are 42 executives in manufacturing, 166 in sales, 21 in advertising, and 33 in all other departments combined. So far, she has consulted with 19 executives from manufacturing, 97 from sales, 9 from advertising, and 18 from the other departments. How many does she still need to consult in *each* department (manufacturing, sales, advertising, and other)?

25) BONUS: Find the digit that A represents.

```
  6417        A = _____
- 3A8
 601A
```

Multiplication

To multiply whole numbers, it is important to line up the numbers according to place values. Neatness is essential.

Example 1:

```
    146
×    29
   1314
    292
   4234
```

- Multiply 9 times each digit in the top number.

  $9 \times 6 = 54$ write 4, carry 5
  $9 \times 4 = 36 + 5 = 41$ write 1, carry 4
  $9 \times 1 = 9 + 4 = 13$ write 3, carry 1
                  write 1 carried

- Multiply 2 times each digit in the top number. Begin writing under tens column because you are now multiplying by a digit in the tens place.

  $2 \times 6 = 12$ write 2, carry 1
  $2 \times 4 = 8 + 1 = 9$ write 9
  $2 \times 1 = 2$ write 2

- Add the products.

Example 2:

```
    36
×   70
     0
   252
  2520
```

- Multiplying 0 times each digit in the top number will yield zero. This can be written in every column but since zero added to any other number equals zero, it is only needed in the ones column.
- Multiply 7 by each digit in the top number and add the products.

Problems   Line problems up vertically before multiplying.

1) $7 \times 10 =$ _____
2) $13 \times 9 =$ _____
3) $11 \times 6 =$ _____
4) $5 \times 7 =$ _____
5) $14 \times 3 =$ _____
6) $19 \times 7 =$ _____
7) $15 \times 15 =$ _____
8) $12 \times 8 =$ _____
9) $16 \times 12 =$ _____
10) $20 \times 14 =$ _____

11)	176 × 92	13)	3,572 × 1,681	15)	864 × 777	17)	147 × 39	19)	4,000 × 2,867
12)	1,487 × 963	14)	293 × 47	16)	2,921 × 2,786	18)	65,814 × 21,493	20)	4,378 × 2,913

21) Cassie is trying to build her regular customer clientele. She has placed newspaper ads in her local paper offering $2 off shampoo, cut, and blow dry and $1 off shampoo and set. She has noticed an increase of customers and has kept accurate records of all new customers. If she had 19 new shampoo, cut, and blow dry customers, how much money did she discount for that service? If she had 18 new shampoo & set customers, how much money did she discount for that service? (These discounts take away from your profit as an operator but they are an excellent way to start advertising your services if you are new to the area.) _____

22) Jennifer Austin is paid by the hour at Forever Yours Hair Salon. How many hours did she work this week if she worked three 8-hour days and two 9-hour days? _____

23) Tracy is considering advertising her new beauty salon on the radio. A 60-second 'spot' (commercial) on WZOA costs $337. How much would eight 60-second spots cost? _____

24) Katie Lee bought new wall decorations for her beauty salon. She bought 6 pictures that cost $21 each, 4 shelves that cost $12 each, and 3 poster prints at $7 each. How much did she spend? _____

Division

To divide whole numbers, place the dividend (number to be divided) under the division sign. Place the divisor (number you're dividing by) to the left of the sign.

Example 1:

$$\begin{array}{r} 27 \\ 64\overline{)1728} \\ -128 \\ \hline 448 \\ -\ 448 \\ \hline 0 \end{array}$$

- Look at the dividend from left to right, choosing a number 64 will divide into.
  - —will 64 divide into 1?   NO
  - —will 64 divide into 17?   NO
  - —will 64 divide into 172?   YES
- Decide how many times 64 will go into 172. (64 × 2 = 128)
- Place the 2 above the last digit in 172. (the 2).
- Write down the 128 and subtract.
- Bring down the next digit after 172 (the 8) and decide how many times 64 will go into 448. (64 × 7 = 448)
- Place the 7 above the 8 in 1728.
- Write down the 448 and subtract.
- In whole number division, the difference after all numbers are brought down is called the *remainder*.
- In this case, the remainder is zero and is not written.

Example 2:

```
        541 R 21
  27 ) 14628
     - 135
        112
      - 108
         48
         27
         21
```

- Look at the dividend from left to right, choosing a number 27 will divide into.
  - —will 27 divide into 1?   NO
  - —will 27 divide into 14?   NO
  - —will 27 divide into 146?   YES
- Decide how many times 27 will go into 146. (27 × 5 = 135)
- Place the 5 above the last digit in 146. (the 6).
- Write down the 135 and subtract.
- Bring down the next digit (2) and decide how many times 27 will go into 112. (27 × 4 = 108)
- Place the 4 above the 2 in 14628.
- Write down the 108 and subtract.
- Bring down the next digit (8) and decide how many times 27 will go into 48. (27 × 1 = 27)
- Place the 1 above the 8 in 14628.
- Write down the 27 and subtract. 21 is the remainder.

Problems   Complete the following division problems. Write the answer and any remainder.

1) 40) 276   _____   11) 149) 30098   _____

2) 14) 294   _____   12) 91) 2910   _____

3) 11) 1346   _____   13) 8) 415   _____

4) 109) 3336   _____   14) 74) 12289   _____

5) 207) 1250   _____   15) 43) 3608   _____

6) 17) 357   _____   16) 80) 48960   _____

7) 84) 1388   _____   17) 78) 7225   _____

8) 25) 389   _____   18) 16) 11568   _____

9) 33) 956   _____   19) 29) 26460   _____

10) 8) 3296   _____   20) 34) 2550   _____

21) Demetria Grimm works as a cosmetologist. Because she is paid a different amount each week (based on how many customers she has and what type of services she completes), she cannot depend on a regular amount for her paycheck from week to week. She decided to average her last six weeks' paychecks to have a better idea how much money she makes in a normal week. The total of the six paychecks is $1,632. What is her average pay for a week?   _____

22) Jessica received some new samples from her sales representative when she placed her supply order yesterday. She has decided to share the samples with all of the operators in her shop so that she can get everyone's opinion about the items. There are seven cosmetologists who work there (including her). How many of the following should each one receive?

a. 203 conditioner packets   _____

b. 98 combs   _____

c. 168 styling gel packets   _____

23) Carole is manager of Nightlife Salon in Greenview Hills. She recently bought a tanning bed for her salon and is trying to determine how long it will be before she has made any profit on it. The tanning bed cost $2,152 and she charges $8 an hour to use it. How many hours of use will it take to pay for the tanning bed?   _____

24) Tammy works in a cooperative salon where all of the expenses required to operate the shop (supplies, utilities, rent, etc.) is shared equally between all operators. If there are six operators in the shop, how much must each one pay for:

a. electricity, if the bill is $144?   _____

b. water, if the bill is $114?   _____

c. rent, if the bill is $1,410 a month?   _____

d. supplies, if the bill is $714?   _____

Mixed Operations

Problems Identify the operations needed to solve the following problems and then solve.

1) Janice works 8 hours a day, 5 days a week. She also works 5 hours on Saturday. How many hours does she work altogether?   _____

2) Brianne takes inventory in the dispensary. In permanent wave kits, she has 6 cases of New Life, 3 cases of PermAction, and 5 cases of Go-between. Each case contains 12 perms.

a. How many of each does she have?   _____

b. How many permanent wave kits does she have altogether?   _____

3) Teresa spent $182 on 13 pamphlet sets for the beauty shop. How much does each pamphlet set cost?   _____

4) Alyse needs 1500 hours to complete her training at Ohio School of Cosmetology. She currently has 319. How many more does she need?   _____

5) Rick bought 7 new uniforms when he completed his manager training. Each uniform costs $21. How much did he spend on uniforms?   _____

6) Sherry missed 7 hours of work due to illness. If she normally works 51 hours a week, how many hours did she work this week?   _____

7) Cathy needs 17 dozen perm rods in each of 8 styling stations. She currently has 78 dozen in stock. How many more should she order?   _____

8) Michael is redecorating his shop. He is taking out all 9 of the shampoo bowls and the 12 styling stations and is ordering new. The supply company will give him a trade-in on the old equipment so that he can buy

the new equipment at a lower price. The cost of a new shampoo bowl is $689 and they will give him a $125 trade-in for an old one. The cost of a styling station is $1,263 and they will give him a $206 trade-in for an old one.

a. How much will he have to pay to replace one bowl?   _____

b. How much will he have to pay to replace all 9 bowls?   _____

c. How much will he have to pay to replace one styling station?   _____

d. How much will he have to pay to replace all 12 styling stations?   _____

e. What is his total bill?   _____

9) Casey McGuire and her fellow employees pay $4 a month into a flower fund at work. There are seven employees altogether. How much money is collected in the flower fund every year?   _____

10) Jackie has determined that she can complete a hair cut every fifteen minutes. How many haircuts can she complete in a five-hour day? (Remember, there are 60 minutes in an hour.)   _____

11) Courtney Houston opens her shop on the following schedule:

Sunday & Monday	CLOSED	Thursday	10–5
Tuesday	10–7	Friday	10–7
Wednesday	10–5	Saturday	10–7

How many hours is she open altogether in a week?   _____

12) Nora decides to buy some new poster prints for the walls of her shop. She decides to get three prints per wall and she has six walls to cover. If each print costs $7, how much will the new prints cost?   _____

13) A box of neck-wrap cotton contains 1250 feet of cotton. If an average customer uses 2 feet of cotton, how many customers will one box take care of?   _____

14) Dana is a cosmetology student. He needs 1400 hours of schooling to get his certificate and be able to take his state board tests. Of that 1400 hours, 600 hours must be in Theory, 400 in Practice, and 400 in Clinical work. How many more hours in each category does he need if he has the following hours?   _____

Theory   492
Practice   371
Clinical   229

15) Lindsey Greer puts $15 each week into a savings account. How much does she save in a year if she makes no withdrawals from the account?   _____

16) Donna is putting in new floor tiles in the reception area of her shop. Each tile is 1 foot square.

a. If the room measures 12 × 14 how many tiles will she need?   _____

b. If the tiles cost $5 for 20 tiles, how much will she pay for the tiles? (Must be purchased in groups of 20 even if she cannot use them all.)   _____

17) Lois is considering buying a washer and dryer for her shop. She currently uses a laundry service for her towels and other items and pays $47 a week for the service. A new washer would cost $482 and a dryer would cost $519.

a. How much would the new washer and dryer cost altogether?   _____

b. How much does it cost to use a laundry service for a year?   _____

c. Even though she would have to purchase her own detergent and electricity to operate her own machines, does purchasing her own equipment appear to be a savings?   _____

Chapter 3

Decimal Operations

When working with decimal numbers in calculations, it is important to understand what significance the decimal has in the number.

In the number 211.65, two hundred eleven is a **whole** number. It represents 211 entire units (of money, if used with a dollar sign.) Every whole number is merely a count of some sort of item. The .65 in 211.65 represents a **part** of a whole unit. For example, in money, $.65 means part of a dollar (indicated by the dollar sign). Sixty-five cents is part of a dollar, but not a whole dollar.

A common mistake is to write .65¢ to mean sixty-five cents. The decimal .65 means a part of a whole and the ¢ symbol means cents. Therefore, .65¢ means part of a cent...not 65 whole cents, but part of 1 cent. The correct way to write sixty-five cents is either $.65 (part of a dollar) or 65¢ (sixty-five whole cents).

Addition

To add decimal numbers, it is important to line up the numbers according to place value (commonly called "lining up on the decimal"). Neatness in lining up the columns will help insure an accurate total.

Once the numbers are lined up correctly, the process of addition is the same as in whole number addition.

Example 1: Add 21.061 + 4.08 + 161.3 + 49

```
|2|1.|0|6|1
| |4.|0|8|
1|6|1.|3| |
 |4|9.| | |
2|3|5.|4|4|1
```

Notice that the decimal is placed in the answer in alignment with where it was in the individual numbers.

Problems   Write the following problems vertically before solving.

1) 8 + 2.06 + 5.353 + 9.99 + 100 =   _____

2) 41 + 8.602 + 9.0009 + 4.16 =   _____

3) .0009 + .009 + .9001 + .009 + .081 =   _____

4) 5 + .5 + .05 + .005 + .0005 =   _____

5) 19 + 216.53 + 8.86 + .0051 =   _____

6) 9.621 + 9001.001 + 46.259 + 8.0001 =   _____

7) 1.03 + .8 + .052 + 9.96 + 211.4 =   _____

8) 4.6 + 6.4 + 8.001 + .05 + 216.003 =   _____

9) $19 + 99.99 + .009 + .001 =$ _____

10) $6 + 71.3 + 48.004 + .5 + .045 + .005 =$ _____

11) Find the total of the following bank deposit: _____

Pennies	.29
Nickels	2.05
Dimes	1.10
Quarters	8.75
$1 bills	48.00
$5 bills	20.00
$10 bills	60.00
$20 bills	80.00
Checks	+ 179.87

12) Clare Blymyer owns Sundance Salon. She recently received a bill for beauty supplies. She checks the total before paying the bill. What should be the total of the following items? _____

Roller End Wraps	$ 22.69
Mexsin Shampoo, 1 case	163.36
Permanent Wave Rods	+ 36.81

13) Complete the following invoice: _____

QTY	ITEM	UNIT COST	EXTENSION
3	Cs. Tint	$17.489	$ 52.467
6	Bx. Plastic Gloves	10.465	62.790
9	Bx. Rollers	17.899	+ 161.091
		TOTAL =	

14) You work at Beauty Manufacturing Corporation in inventory control. You need to total the following inventory for the secretarial office: _____

3	Desks	$ 679.98
3	Secretarial Chairs	308.81
3	Wastebaskets	21.17
3	Desk Lamps	43.55
3	File Cabinets	654.04
1	Stapler	6.14
1	Tape Dispenser	+ 3.16

15) Karen Harshbarger lives in a state that has a tax rate of 3.5%. This means she pays 3.5% of her income each year for taxes. Next year, the tax rate will increase by .025%. What will the new tax rate be? _____

16) Danielle Compton pays her employees once a week. Below is a copy of last week's payroll. Total the amount she paid her employees last week. _____

Kate Manwell	$ 266.36
Abbey Jackson-Smith	361.13
Douglas Nieman	176.38
Gretta Brown	244.73
Brenda Loller	271.07
Olivia Trent	+ 378.23

17) Hannah Mason closes Nightingale Beauty Shop every evening during the week. Part of her responsibilities in closing the shop includes making the bank deposit. Total the bank deposit for each evening:

a. Tuesday

pennies	.35
nickels	1.65
dimes	.70
quarters	3.00
$1 dollar bills	16.00
$5 dollar bills	35.00
$10 dollar bills	50.00
$20 dollar bills	160.00
checks	57.95

_____

b. Wednesday

pennies	.41
nickels	.95
dimes	2.20
quarters	2.25
$1 dollar bills	13.00
$5 dollar bills	30.00
$10 dollar bills	80.00
$20 dollar bills	140.00
checks	51.73

_____

c. Thursday

pennies	.79
nickels	6.70
dimes	4.70
quarters	15.75
$1 dollar bills	113.00
$5 dollar bills	205.00
$10 dollar bills	190.00
$20 dollar bills	260.00
checks	89.26

_____

d. Friday

pennies	.14
nickels	.60
dimes	2.00
quarters	3.75
$1 dollar bills	7.00
$5 dollar bills	50.00
$10 dollar bills	90.00
$20 dollar bills	40.00
checks	153.74

_____

Subtraction

In subtraction of decimal numbers it is again important to line up the numbers according to place value.

Once the numbers are lined up correctly, the process of subtraction is the same as in whole number subtraction. One exception, however, is when the minuend (number from which you are subtracting) holds fewer place values than the subtrahend (number being subtracted).

Example 1:   1.06   minuend — fewer place values
                   − 0.1742

In this case, it is necessary to use zeros as place holders:

$$
\begin{array}{r}
1.0600 \\
-\ 0.1742 \\
\hline
0.8858
\end{array}
$$

This gives us the ability to borrow and solve the subtraction.

Problems   Line up vertically according to place values, then subtract.

1)   48.6 − 21.831 = _____   6)   23.4 − 23.04 = _____

2)   6 − 3.91 = _____   7)   100 − 99.99 = _____

3)   8.999 − 7.983 = _____   8)   4.44 − 0.06 = _____

4)   5.52 − 4.116 = _____   9)   1753.8 − 9.9 = _____

5)   8963.8 − 2.0004 = _____   10)   652.9 − 651.667 = _____

11)   Steve Morrison made a deposit of $1640.00 into a savings account. On March 6 he withdrew $110.87. What is his new balance?   _____

12)   Rae Ann charges $27.95 for a permanent wave. One customer gave her $30 and told her to keep the change as a tip. What was the amount of her tip?   _____

13)   Catherine Blake recently paid $17.59 for a new pair of scissors. Later that same day she found the same brand of scissors on sale at another store for $16.95. How much could she have saved by buying the other pair?   _____

14)   Find the difference in the following two list prices.

    File Folders (Aplar brand) $4.528/doz.
    File Folders (Jaguar brand)   4.67/doz.   _____

15)   Kristine Wagner works at Marie's Cosmetics. She often makes small purchases from salesmen, pays for package deliveries, buys stamps, and makes other purchases out of a petty cash fund. This week the petty cash fund started out with $25. She paid $3.64 for a package delivery and $5.91 for a cosmetic sample purchased from a salesman. Later in the week she paid $.75 for a poster to hang in the window of the store. What is the balance of the petty cash fund after these three purchases?   _____

16)   Jack Taylor is a student at Illinois Beauty Academy. He is paying his tuition on a monthly basis. His total bill is $3567 and he has paid $3167.89 so far. How much of his bill remains unpaid?   _____

17)   Fayla Gomez wanted to build an addition to her beauty shop. She consulted two building contractors and asked them for an estimate of the cost to build the addition. Green Brothers Builders would charge $5,566 for the addition and Williams Contracting would charge $5,613.75. Which builder charges less and by how much?   _____

Multiplication

To multiply decimal numbers, it is not necessary to line up the place values. Instead, write the numbers so that they align on the right:

Example 1: 19.6 × 2.01

$$\begin{array}{r} 19.6 \\ \times \quad 2.01 \end{array}$$

The process of multiplication is the same as in whole number multiplication except that when you have completed the multiplication, it is necessary to place the decimal in your answer.

<table>
<tr><td>

$$\begin{array}{r} 19.6 \\ \times \quad 2.01 \\ \hline 196 \\ 000 \\ \underline{392} \\ 39396 \end{array}$$

</td><td>

$$\begin{array}{r} 19.\mathbf{6} \\ \times \quad 2.\mathbf{01} \\ \hline 196 \\ 000 \\ \underline{392} \\ 39.\mathbf{396} \end{array}$$

</td><td>

• A total of 3 numbers to the right of the decimal

• should be the same in the answer

</td></tr>
</table>

Problems   Line up vertically, then multiply and place the decimal in the answer.

1) 6.007 x .001 = _____

2) 9.72 x 14.6 = _____

3) 48.64 x 5.3 = _____

4) 9.61 x 8.14 = _____

5) 8.081 x .005 = _____

6) 9.9 x 8.76 = _____

7) 1463 x 5.7 = _____

8) 59.232 x 14.8 = _____

9) 11.652 x 7.7 = _____

10) 436.49 x 2.117 = _____

11) Shane Fayler earns $8.75 an hour as a cosmetologist at a day care center for the elderly. He worked 55 hours last week. What is his total pay for the week?   _____

12) To find the area of a room it is necessary to multiply length by width. Jack Hillburn needs to find the area of his shop to order floor covering. What is the area of his shop if the dimensions are 18.5' x 12.625'?   _____

13) Kayla Hardesty sells beauty supplies. Complete the following invoice.

QTY	ITEM	UNIT COST	EXTENSION
2	179-2 foundation	$ 7.48	_____
1	9-3 lipstick	6.51	_____
3	473-6 mascara	7.80	_____

14) Angela Gordensen pays for child care for her three children while she works. The daily rate per child is $7.50. How much does she pay each day for child care? How much does she pay for a five-day week?   _____

15) Johnna Keelor manages Festida Beauty Salon. At the end of each week she determines the total hours worked for each person and reports the hours to the main office of Festida Beauty Salons International.

Empl. #	Days	Length of Shift (hrs.)	Total
17	5	8.5	_____
11	5	6.75	_____
13	4	10	_____
14	6	5.25	_____

16) Karen Oliphant recently bought some advertising time on a local television station for her new beauty shop. She paid $279.85 for each 30-second commercial. How much will she pay altogether for six 30-second commercials?   _____

17) Greg Nelson pays $129.47 a month for business insurance to protect his barber shop from fire, theft, storm, and other damage. How much does he pay for an entire year's protection?   _____

Division

To divide decimal numbers, it is necessary to convert the divisor (number being divided by) to a whole number. To do so, you can move the decimal to the right until it is at the right of the number.

Example 1:   1954.66 ÷ 5.67 =

1) First, set up the problem under a division sign.

   5.67) 1954.66

2) Then, move the decimal in the divisor (5.67) to the right.

   5.67) 1954.66   becomes   567) 1954.66

Changing 5.67 to 567 is accomplished by moving the decimal, but it is actually the process of multiplying 5.67 by 100. (5.67 × 100 = 567) This same multiplication must be done on the dividend (number being divided) for the result to be correct.

3) Next, change the dividend by multiplying (by 100 in this case.)

   1954.66 × 100 = 195466

This is the same as moving the decimal the same number of places in the dividend as you did in the divisor.

   567) 1954.66   becomes   567) 195466

4) Once the decimal has been moved out of the divisor and moved by similar multiplication in the dividend, division is completed as in whole number division.

```
          344.737          • division is completed to the thousandths place so that
567. ) 195466.                 rounding can be done to the 100ths place
     − 1701
       2536
     − 2268
       2686
     − 2268
       4180               • zero place holder
     − 3969
       2110               • zero place holder
     − 1701
       4090               • zero place holder
     − 3969
        121
```

ANSWER: 344.74 after rounding

Instead of having a remainder if the division does not come out evenly, it is common to continue division with the use of zero place holders. If it does not come out evenly then, it will be necessary to round the answer to some designated place value. If a place value is specified in the problem, follow that guideline. If not, it is acceptable to round the answer to the hundredths place.

Problems   Remove the decimal from the divisor by moving it to the right. Then move the decimal in the dividend in the same manner (by moving the same number of decimal places as in divisor). Then, divide as in whole number division and round to the hundredths place.

1) 36.22) 56.374 _____   6) 4.2) 2893.8 _____

2) 264.1) 784.4 _____   7) 80.5) 336.1 _____

3) 5.1) 1201.05 _____   8) 78.4) 163.2 _____

4) 4.6) 741.4 _____   9) 3.6) 82.4 _____

5) 223.4) 1797 _____   10) 486.325) 3755.8 _____

11) If a bottle of nail polish usually yields 30 manicures, applying it to all ten nails with a double coat, and the bottle costs $2.59, how much does the polish cost for each manicure?   _____

12) Helen Jackson recently bought 125 combs that were imprinted with her shop name and is giving them away to her customers. The total bill came to $7.81. How much does each comb cost?   _____

13) Jennifer was recently asked on a questionaire how much money she makes per hour. Since she is paid commission she does not have a set rate that she earns per hour. Help her to find the average amount that she makes in an hour with the following information.   _____

Monday	7.5 hours	$125.50
Tuesday	8 hours	110.95
Wednesday	8 hours	86.00
Thursday	6.5 hours	50.00
Friday	10.5 hours	167.75

14) Find the average cost of a permanent wave in Plainville if the six salons charge the following prices: $25.95, $31.99, $15.95, $20.00, $29.99, and $30.95.   _____

15) Brand A polish remover costs $5.67 for 25 oz. and Brand B costs $6.14 for 28 oz. To find the better buy (assuming quality is the same), you first must find the unit cost of each item. To do this, divide the cost by the number of ounces.

a. What is the unit cost of Brand A per ounce?   _____

b. What is the unit cost of Brand B per ounce?   _____

c. Which is cheaper?   _____

Mixed Operations

Problems   Complete the following decimal operations problems by first determining what operations must be done and then solving the problem. More than one step may be required.

1) Shannon Brown was asked to find the average weight of the supply shipments being sent from her department at Weger Beauty Supply Company. Find the average of the following.   _____

   76.33, 26.76, 1.7, 347, 678.33, 15, 467.87, 582.49, 35.2, 32.87, 26.8, 485.05

2) Tim Normandy bought a new uniform from Halsey Uniforms for $26.79 plus tax. If sales tax is found by multiplying the cost of the items by .065, what is the sales tax? What is the total cost of the uniform including tax?   _____

3) Brian Hudson heard that the barber staff at Golliver Hospital earns $13.57 per hour. He is currently earning $12.66 per hour at his job in a salon. How much more could he earn per hour at Golliver than at his current job?   _____

4) Natalie Greenwood drives 5.7 miles one way to work each day. Gasoline costs $1.09 per gallon and she can drive 34.2 miles on a gallon of gas. How much does one day's drive to and from work cost her for gasoline?   _____

5) Raphael Bonnare orders supplies for his salon. He compares the cost of shampoo from two different companies. Gladwell Inc. sells Texin shampoo $11.79 for 20 oz. Frampton's Supply sells the shampoo for $13.55 for 25 oz.

   a. What is the unit cost of Gladwell's shampoo per ounce?   _____

   b. What is the unit cost of Frampton's shampoo per ounce?   _____

   c. Which one is least expensive and by how much?   _____

6) Phil bought 4 textbooks at University Book Store. His total bill was $57.92. What was the average cost of the books?   _____

7) Joanne drives 17.8 miles to work, 5.2 miles from there to her evening college class, and 16.2 miles from there back home. What is her total driving distance each day?   _____

8) Cherie Preston used a 28.25 oz. jar of cold cream for her permanent wave customers. If each customer received an equal amount of cream and the jar lasted through 65 customers, how many ounces was used on each customer?   _____

9) Daniel Douglas found a sale on a hair dryer/diffuser that he needed to buy. The original cost was $69.75 and the sale price was $59.98. How much did he save by buying the hair dryer/diffuser on sale?   _____

10) Sarah needs to complete 103 more hours for her cosmetology training. How many hours would she need to complete each week to finish the course in four weeks?

_____

11) Mary Anne Wilson keeps track of her wages each week. During October, she earned the following amounts: week 1 — $613.53; week 2 — $365.26; week 3 — $511.17; week 4 — $491.87. What is her total wage for the month of October? What is the average of the four weeks' wages?

_____

12) Patty Ford has a list of 109 regular customers. She likes to send each one of these customers a card at the holidays to thank them for their patronage during the past year.

a. If cards cost $1.99 for 14 cards, how much will she pay for cards? (She must buy the entire box even if she cannot use all fourteen cards.)

_____

b. What is the postage required to send 109 cards if each card requires a $.29 stamp?

_____

c. What is the total Patty will spend for this advertising?

_____

13) Tricia Phillips wants to find the total amount she spends on business-related expenses in her work as a cosmetologist. In a six-month time period, she kept track of the following expenses: 3 pr. navy blue pants ($16.99 each), 5 red smocks ($14.79 each), 1 pr. white nursing shoes ($37.99 each), new scissors ($18.99), a set of appointment cards (100 purchased for a total of $7.50), and miscellaneous beauty supplies (she has bills for these in the amounts of $15.99, $3.29, and $27.91).

a. What is her total business-related expenses for the past six months?

_____

b. What is the average amount she spends each month on business-related expenses?

_____

14) Brenda Calhoun is planning to return to school for manager's training. She has the option of going to Precision Beauty School in Ralston or to Hohman's Beauty Academy in nearby Covington. The cost of tuition at Precision is $2,150 and she would travel 30 miles a day (round trip). The cost of tuition at Hohman's is $2,590 and she would travel 7 miles a day (round trip). The training should take approximately 15 weeks, five days a week, at either school and the cost per mile to drive is $.24.

a. What is the travel cost for attending Precision?

_____

b. What is the total cost for attending Precision?

_____

c. What is the travel cost for attending Hohman's?

_____

d. What is the total cost for attending Hohman's?

_____

e. Which is less expensive?

_____

Chapter 4

Fraction Operations

Fractions are used in a wide variety of ways in cosmetology. Hours of training are generally recorded as a fraction. Simple office procedures such as payroll or ordering often contain fractions. The more familiar you are with fraction operations, the better equipped you will be for your job in cosmetology.

Defining a Fraction

What is a fraction? A fraction is a symbolic way of writing a **part** of something. Just as the decimal $.65 shows **part** of a dollar, so $\frac{7}{8}$ lb. shows **part** of a pound.

A fraction can be written in two different ways: $\frac{7}{8}$ or 7/8.

A fraction is made up of two parts, the numerator and the denominator. The numerator is the top number (or first number) and it signifies how many parts of the whole are being represented by the fraction. The denominator is the bottom number (or second number) and it signifies how many parts the whole has been divided or sectioned into.

For example, in $\frac{7}{8}$ the number 7 is the numerator and 8 is the denominator. The fraction $\frac{7}{8}$ means that 7 parts out of 8 possible are being represented. If you have an order containing 8 cases of beauty supplies and 7 have arrived, you have 7 cases out of the 8 that could possibly be sent. You have $\frac{7}{8}$ of the order.

Another example is in money. If you have only 1 quarter, you have 1 quarter out of the 4 that you would need to equal a dollar. The fraction to represent this is 1/4 or $\frac{1}{4}$. You have one-fourth ($\frac{1}{4}$) of a dollar.

Or imagine that you were supposed to use 3 oz. of cleaning solution and each bottle contained 6 oz. You need 3 oz. out of 6 oz. available or $\frac{3}{6}$. A fraction can be reduced if the numerator and denominator have a number in common that will equally divide into each. In this case, 3 will divide into 3 and also into 6.

$$\frac{3}{6} \div \frac{3}{3} = \frac{1}{2}$$

You would use $\frac{1}{2}$ a bottle.

Least Common Denominators

To compare two fractions, it is necessary that both fractions have the same denominator. Remember that the denominator shows how many parts the whole has been divided or sectioned into. Once the two fractions have the same denominator, it is possible to look at the numerators to decide which fraction is larger. For example, $\frac{5}{8}$ and $\frac{3}{8}$ have the same denominator. Let these fractions represent the time you have worked out of an 8 hour shift. The first fraction indicates that you have worked 5 hours out of 8 possible. The second fraction indicates that you have worked 3 hours out of 8 possible. Which time period is longer, 5 hours or 3 hours? It is easy to see that 5 hours is the larger time period. But if the shifts had not both been equally divided into eight 1-hour periods, comparison would have been more difficult.

It is possible to create like denominators for fractions. The process of doing so is called finding the **least common denominator** (LCD). A least common denominator between two or more fractions is the smallest number possible which all of the available denominators can divide into. For example, in the fractions $\frac{1}{2}$ and $\frac{2}{5}$, 2 and 5 are the denominators. Since they are not like denominators (the same number) we must find the least common denominator. The question we must ask is: What is the smallest number that 2 and 5 can both divide into?

Multiples of 2: 2 4 6 8 **10**

Multiples of 5: 5 **10**

Ten is the smallest number that 2 and 5 will both divide into. Therefore, ten is the least common denominator for $\frac{1}{2}$ and $\frac{3}{5}$.

Finding the least common denominator of two or more fractions is the key to being able to compare. Having the LCD is also necessary in addition or subtraction of fractions. Let's look more closely at how to find the LCD.

Example 1: Find the LCD of $\frac{4}{6}$ and $\frac{7}{9}$.

1) You are trying to find the smallest number that the denominators 6 and 9 will both divide evenly into.
2) Look at the multiples of 6 and of 9 until you find a number in common. (Finding the multiples of a number is the same as counting by that number.)

Multiples of 6: 6 12 **18**

Multiples of 9: 9 **18**

3) 18 is the least common denominator.

Example 2: Find the LCD of $\frac{3}{7}$ and $\frac{5}{8}$.

Multiples of 7: 7 14 21 28 35 42 49 **56**

Multiples of 8: 8 16 24 32 40 48 **56**

The least common denominator of $\frac{3}{7}$ and $\frac{5}{8}$ is 56.

Example 3: Find the LCD of $\frac{1}{12}$ and $\frac{5}{6}$.

Multiples of 12: **12**

Multiples of 6: 6 **12**

The least common denominator of $\frac{1}{12}$ and $\frac{5}{6}$ is 12.

We can use the least common denominator (LCD) to help us compare the fractions $\frac{1}{2}$ and $\frac{3}{5}$. We will make 10 the new denominator in both fractions.

Since the denominator must be 10, we will multiply the denominator of the original fraction by 5 to result in 10. Since the denominator has been multiplied by five, the numerator must be multiplied by five also. This will produce a fraction equal to $\frac{1}{2}$. **Equal fractions** are fractions where the numerator and denominator of 1 fraction can be multiplied by the same number to result in the second fraction.

What you are really doing when you multiply numerator and denominator both by 5 is shown here:

$$\frac{1 \times 5}{2 \times 5} = \frac{5}{10}$$

Note that $\frac{5}{5}$ is really the whole number 1.
You are simply multiplying by one.

In $\frac{3}{5}$, the five in the denominator must be multiplied by two to result in 10. Thus, the numerator will also be multiplied by 2.

$$\frac{3 \times 2}{5 \times 2} = \frac{6}{10}$$

Note that $\frac{2}{2}$ is equivalent to one.
Thus, you are really multiplying by 1.

Now you can compare $\frac{1}{2}$ and $\frac{3}{5}$. ($\frac{1}{2} = \frac{5}{10}$ and $\frac{3}{5} = \frac{6}{10}$) $\frac{5}{10}$ and $\frac{6}{10}$ can be compared easily. Since 6 parts is more than 5 parts, $\frac{6}{10}$ is larger. Therefore, $\frac{3}{5}$ is larger than $\frac{1}{2}$.

Example 4: Find the LCD of $\frac{1}{6}$ and $\frac{3}{8}$ and then convert each fraction to an equal fraction using the LCD.

1) Find the LCD.

Multiples of 6: 6 12 18 **24**

Multiples of 8: 8 16 **24**

2) Make the LCD the new denominator in each fraction and determine the new numerator for each by multiplication.

$$\frac{1}{6} = \frac{?}{24} \qquad 6 \times ? = 24$$
$$6 \times 4 = 24$$

So, multiply the 1 × 4 to get 4 as the new numerator.

$$\frac{1}{6} = \frac{4}{24}$$

$$\frac{3}{8} = \frac{?}{24} \qquad 8 \times ? = 24$$
$$8 \times 3 = 24$$

So, multiply the 3 x 3 to get 9 as the new numerator.

$$\frac{3}{8} = \frac{9}{24}$$

The LCD is 24 and the new fractions are $\frac{1}{6} = \frac{4}{24}$ and $\frac{3}{8} = \frac{9}{24}$.

Example 5: Find the LCD for $\frac{4}{5}$, $\frac{3}{9}$, and $\frac{5}{6}$.

Multiples of 5: 5 10 15 20 25 30 35 40 45 50

Multiples of 9: 9 18 27 36 45 54 63 72 81 90

Multiples of 6: 6 12 18 24 30 36 42 48 54 60

After a considerable list a LCD still is not found. Be sure you haven't made a mistake and keep trying.

Multiples of 5: 5 10 15 20 25 30 35 40 45 50 55 60 65 70 75 80 85 **90** 95

Multiples of 9: 9 18 27 36 45 54 63 72 81 **90**

Multiples of 6: 6 12 18 24 30 36 42 48 54 60 66 72 78 84 **90** 96

The LCD is 90.

Problems   Find the LCD for the following pairs or groups of fractions.

1) 4/5, 6/7 _____

2) 3/8, 1/6 _____

3) 7/10, 4/5 _____

4) 3/8, 2/5 _____

5) 7/12, 7/8 _____

6) 2/3, 6/8 _____

7) 5/8, 3/10, 1/2 _____

8) 9/10, 5/7 _____

9) 3/4, 5/6, 2/5 _____

10) 1/4, 5/6, 3/8 _____

In #11–#15 find the LCD and then convert each fraction to an equal fraction using the LCD.

11) $\dfrac{3}{7}$

$\dfrac{11}{12}$

12) $\dfrac{9}{10}$

$\dfrac{5}{6}$

13) $\dfrac{2}{3}$

$\dfrac{4}{9}$

14) $\dfrac{1}{6}$

$\dfrac{3}{8}$

15) $\dfrac{4}{5}$

$\dfrac{7}{12}$

In #16–#20 compare the fractions and determine which is largest.

16) 5/7, 3/4   _____

17) 6/9, 5/6   _____

18) 12/15, 9/10   _____

19) 5/6, 4/7   _____

20) 3/5, 4/6   _____

Reducing Fractions

Often in working with fractions it is necessary to reduce fractions. Reducing a fraction involves dividing both the numerator and denominator by the largest number that will divide evenly into both (**greatest common factor — GCF**). For example, in $\frac{10}{40}$ the factors of ten are 1, 2, 5, and 10 and the factors of forty are 1, 2, 4, 5, 8, and 10. The factors that ten and forty have in common are: 2, 5, and 10. Which of these is the greatest? Ten is the greatest common factor. Thus, this fraction can be reduced by dividing the numerator and denominator both by 10.

$$\frac{10 \div 10}{40 \div 10} = \frac{1}{4}$$

Another method of reducing numbers does not require finding the greatest common factor. To reduce a fraction without finding the GCF simply divide the numerator and denominator by any number that will divide evenly into both. Continue to do this until there are no other numbers that will divide evenly into both. For example, in the $\frac{10}{40}$ problem, you could:

$$\frac{10 \div 2}{40 \div 2} = \frac{5 \div 5}{20 \div 5} = \frac{1}{4}$$

There are more steps but it eliminates the need to find the GCF.

Problems Reduce the following fractions to lowest terms (meaning that there are no other numbers that will divide evenly into the numerator and denominator when you are done.)

1) 6/48 _____

2) 3/9 _____

3) 5/20 _____

4) 8/12 _____

5) 9/54 _____

6) 14/21 _____

7) 6/21 _____

8) 9/15 _____

9) 12/18 _____

10) 8/18 _____

11) 8/20 _____

12) 9/24 _____

13) 10/34 _____

14) 15/33 _____

15) 9/12 _____

16) 8/14 _____

17) 4/18 _____

18) 3/42 _____

19) 2/16 _____

20) 7/28 _____

Mixed Numbers and Improper Fractions

A **mixed number** is a combination of a whole number and a fraction written together. For example, Joyce got $3\frac{1}{2}$ books read from the assignment. Or, Steve completed $4\frac{1}{5}$ customer information records before his break. In each of these examples, the whole number indicates the number of complete (whole) activities accomplished and the fraction indicates that part of another activity was accomplished, but not a whole.

An **improper fraction** is a fraction where the numerator is larger than the denominator. For example, the number $\frac{7}{2}$ is an improper fraction as is $\frac{21}{5}$.

When writing numbers in lowest terms it is necessary to change any improper fractions to a mixed number. This is a process of dividing the denominator into the numerator to find out how many **whole** groups there are—this would be the whole number. Then the remainder that is left after division, if any, is the number of **parts** left and this becomes the numerator of the fraction.

Example 1: Change $\frac{7}{2}$ to a mixed number.

1) We will first divide 7 by 2.

$$\begin{array}{r} 3 \\ 2\overline{)7} \\ -6 \\ \hline 1 \end{array}$$

• The whole number is 3. There are three **whole** groups of 2 in the number 7.

• The remainder is 1. The **part** that is left is 1 out of 2 possible or $\frac{1}{2}$.

$\frac{7}{2}$ becomes $3\frac{1}{2}$. There are 3 groups of 2 ($3 \times 2 = 6$) in seven and there is 1 left over ($7 - 6 = 1$)—1 part of a group of 2. Thus, $3\frac{1}{2}$.

Sometimes it is necessary to change a mixed number back to an improper fraction. This is necessary when working with some fraction operations, such as multiplication and division. The procedure for changing a mixed number to an improper fraction is the opposite of what you did in Example 1. For division you divide to see how many times 2 will go into 7 equally, then you subtract to find the remainder. To "undo" this, first, you will multiply the denominator (2) by the whole number (3) to get six total parts (3 groups of 2). Then, you will add the extra part (the remainder 1) on to the six. ($6 + 1 = 7$) You have 7 parts which should be in groups of 2. Thus the improper fraction $\frac{7}{2}$.

Example 2:   Change $4\frac{1}{5}$ to an improper fraction.

1)   You have 4 whole groups of 5 (4 x 5 = 20). Add the extra part (the numerator 1) on to the 20. (20 + 1 = 21) You have 21 parts which should be in groups of 5. Thus, the improper fraction $\frac{21}{5}$.

Another way of looking at these type of problems is shown in the next example.

Example 3:   Change $5\frac{1}{3}$ to an improper fraction, Figure 4-1.

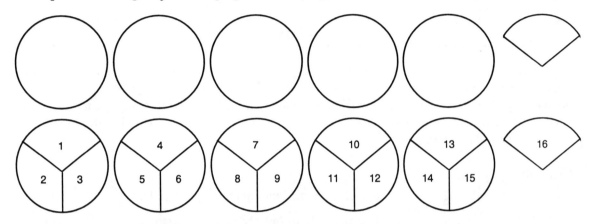

To change $5\frac{1}{3}$ to an improper fraction, multiply the 5 by three to determine the number of thirds that five separates into. Then add the 1 additional third. (5 × 3 = 15 + 1 = 16 thirds)

$$5\ \frac{1}{3} = \frac{16}{3}$$

FIGURE 4-1

Problems   Change these mixed numbers to improper fractions.

1) $4\frac{2}{7}$ _____   11) $4\frac{1}{3}$ _____

2) $1\frac{1}{2}$ _____   12) $6\frac{1}{4}$ _____

3) $5\frac{2}{6}$ _____   13) $3\frac{5}{6}$ _____

4) $6\frac{2}{3}$ _____   14) $5\frac{1}{5}$ _____

5) $3\frac{1}{4}$ _____   15) $2\frac{7}{9}$ _____

6) $3\frac{1}{6}$ _____   16) $7\frac{2}{5}$ _____

7) $6\frac{1}{3}$ _____   17) $4\frac{3}{4}$ _____

8) $4\frac{1}{7}$ _____   18) $1\frac{1}{6}$ _____

9) $10\frac{3}{8}$ _____   19) $4\frac{3}{7}$ _____

10) $3\frac{7}{10}$ _____   20) $3\frac{1}{3}$ _____

In #21–#40, change the following improper fractions to mixed numbers and reduce to lowest terms.

21) $\frac{15}{4}$ _____   25) $\frac{42}{5}$ _____

22) $\frac{18}{14}$ _____   26) $\frac{19}{3}$ _____

23) $\frac{22}{5}$ _____   27) $\frac{16}{7}$ _____

24) $\frac{5}{2}$ _____   28) $\frac{31}{6}$ _____

29) $\frac{14}{7}$ _____   35) $\frac{55}{6}$ _____

30) $\frac{6}{4}$ _____   36) $\frac{19}{2}$ _____

31) $\frac{16}{3}$ _____   37) $\frac{18}{5}$ _____

32) $\frac{25}{4}$ _____   38) $\frac{38}{4}$ _____

33) $\frac{40}{3}$ _____   39) $\frac{45}{2}$ _____

34) $\frac{53}{20}$ _____   40) $\frac{23}{7}$ _____

Addition

To add fractions, it is first necessary to have like denominators (as we used in comparing fractions). Then, once the denominators are the same, you can add the numerators together to find the total number of parts in the whole. Occasionally, the total in the numerator will exceed the number in the denominator. When this occurs, you have an improper fraction. This must then be written in lowest terms as a mixed number.

Example 1:   Add $\frac{5}{6} + \frac{2}{15}$

$$\begin{array}{cc} \frac{5}{6} & \frac{25}{30} \\ \frac{2}{+ \ 15} & \frac{4}{30} \\ & \frac{29}{30} \end{array}$$

- First, change the denominators to the LCD.
- Then, multiply to find the new numerators.
- Next, add the numerators together and leave the denominator alone. Reduce if possible.

Example 2:   Add $\frac{4}{5} + \frac{7}{8}$

$$\begin{array}{cc} \frac{4}{5} & \frac{32}{40} \\ \frac{7}{+ \ 8} & \frac{35}{40} \\ & \frac{67}{40} \\ & 1\frac{27}{40} \end{array}$$

- First, change the denominators to the LCD.
- Then, multiply to find the new numerators.
- Next, add the numerators together and leave the denominator alone. Reduce this fraction because it is an improper fraction. ($67 \div 40 = 1$ remainder 27)

Sometimes, adding fractions includes adding mixed numbers as well, either with another mixed number or with a proper fraction. The addition process for the fractions is the same. If the answer is an improper fraction, it still needs to be converted to a mixed number first. Then the whole number that that creates is carried over and added with the other whole numbers.

Example 3:   Add $4\frac{7}{8} + 2\frac{3}{4}$

$$\begin{array}{rcl} 4\frac{7}{8} & = & 4\frac{7}{8} \\ + \ 2\frac{3}{4} & = & 2\frac{6}{8} \\ & & 6\frac{13}{8} \\ & & \frac{5}{8} \\ & & 7\frac{5}{8} \end{array}$$

- First, change the denominators to the LCD.
- Then, multiply to find the new numerators.
- Next, add the numerators together and leave the denominator alone. Reduce this fraction because it is an improper fraction. ($13 \div 8 = 1$ [one more whole number] remainder 5)
- Carry the whole number 1 over to the whole numbers and add all whole numbers together.
- ($7\frac{5}{8}$ is the final answer)

Problems Add the following pairs or groups of fractions, and write the final answer in lowest terms.

1) $3\dfrac{6}{10}$

   $+\ 5\dfrac{1}{3}$
   _____

3) $\dfrac{12}{14}$

   $+\ 7\dfrac{7}{10}$
   _____

5) $\dfrac{8}{9}$

   $+\ 2\dfrac{7}{12}$
   _____

7) $\dfrac{3}{10}$

   $+\ \dfrac{3}{4}$
   _____

9) $7\dfrac{4}{5}$

   $+\ \dfrac{5}{8}$
   _____

2) $\dfrac{14}{15}$

   $+\ \dfrac{4}{6}$
   _____

4) $\dfrac{9}{14}$

   $+\ 14\dfrac{13}{21}$
   _____

6) $\dfrac{11}{12}$

   $+\ \dfrac{8}{15}$
   _____

8) $\dfrac{10}{12}$

   $+\ \dfrac{5}{21}$
   _____

10) $\dfrac{13}{14}$

   $+\ 8\dfrac{4}{7}$
   _____

11) Shiloh Hair Care Center recently bought Sally's Beauty Salon. They must complete a new inventory showing the total amount of various products on hand. Add the following two inventories together: _____

Permanent Waves	$16\frac{1}{2}$ cases	$12\frac{1}{4}$ cases
Hair Coloring	$15\frac{1}{8}$ cases	$9\frac{1}{4}$ cases
Combs	$22\frac{1}{9}$ cases	$11\frac{1}{5}$ cases
End Wraps	$115\frac{1}{5}$ packages	27 packages
Cotton	$1041\frac{1}{12}$ feet	$316\frac{1}{3}$ feet

12) Karen is completing her cosmetology training. She needs 400 hours of clinical work, 400 hours of theory, and 200 hours of practice. Her totals going into this week were: $387\frac{1}{4}$ clinical, $388\frac{1}{8}$ theory, and 196 practice. This week she completed the following: $13\frac{1}{8}$ clinical, $11\frac{3}{4}$ theory, and $4\frac{1}{12}$ practice. What are her new totals? Does she have the time in every area that is required of her?   _____

13) Jeffrey sells supplies to local beauty shops. Today he handed out samples of a new unbreakable comb to several shops in the Bridgetown area. What is the total quantity of combs that he gave away if he gave the following: $\frac{1}{8}$ case, $\frac{1}{2}$ case, $\frac{1}{12}$ case, $\frac{1}{5}$ case and $\frac{3}{4}$ case?   _____

14) Kelsey Kramer must add up her time sheet to be sent to the State Board of Cosmetology.   Add the following weeks work for her:

Date	Lecture & Theory	Hr	Demonstration	Hr	Practice	Hr	Clinic	Hr
10/7	haircutting	1 ¼	haircutting	½	haircutting	2 ½		
	shampoo	¼	shampoo	¼	shampoo	½		
	scalp care	1 ¾			hairstyling	¾		
	Totals							

FIGURE 4-2 Time sheet adding fractions

Subtraction

To subtract fractions, it is first necessary to have like denominators (as we used in comparing fractions and in addition of fractions). Then, once the denominators are the same, you can subtract the numerators to find the difference. Occasionally, the two numerators cannot be subtracted because the bottom one is larger than the top one from which it is being subtracted. When this occurs, you must borrow from the whole number on top.

Borrowing in fractions is quite a bit different than borrowing in whole numbers. In regular whole number subtraction, you borrow from the tens column to increase the value of the ones column. For example:

$$\begin{array}{r} 1\ 15 \\ \not{2}\not{5} \\ -\ 18 \\ \hline \end{array}$$

- borrowing 1 from the 2 in the tens column allowed you to increase the 5 in the ones column to 15 (which is five plus the ten borrowed)

In fraction borrowing however you borrow from a whole number to increase the numerator of the top fraction. When you borrow 1 from the whole number, you are really borrowing all of the parts of 1 whole unit. For example, you might be borrowing 4 parts of a unit that is sectioned into fourths ($\frac{4}{4}$) or 7 parts of a unit that is sectioned into sevenths ($\frac{7}{7}$). You are borrowing a whole unit regardless of how it is sectioned or divided up.

Example 1:

$$5\frac{1}{6} \qquad 4\frac{7}{6}$$
$$-2\frac{5}{6} \qquad 2\frac{5}{6}$$
$$\overline{} \qquad \overline{2\frac{2}{6}}$$
$$\qquad\qquad 2\frac{1}{3}$$

- First, recognize that $\frac{1}{6} - \frac{5}{6}$ cannot be subtracted.
- Next, borrow one from the 5 and change that one that is borrowed to 6 parts of a unit that is sectioned into sixths (Why sixths? Because that is the common denominator of the problem.)
- Then add the $\frac{6}{6}$ (six sixths borrowed) to the $\frac{1}{6}$ already available ($\frac{6}{6} + \frac{1}{6} = \frac{7}{6}$).
- $\frac{7}{6}$ is large enough to complete the subtraction problem ($\frac{7}{6} - \frac{5}{6} = \frac{2}{6}$).
- Reduce the fraction if necessary.
- Final answer is $2\frac{1}{3}$.

Be sure when subtracting fractions that you put the problem in like denominators first before deciding whether or not to borrow.

Example 2:

$$3\frac{1}{9} \qquad 3\frac{4}{36}$$
$$-1\frac{3}{4} \qquad 1\frac{27}{36}$$
$$\overline{} \qquad \overline{}$$
$$\qquad \overset{2}{\not{3}}\frac{40}{36}$$
$$\qquad -1\frac{27}{36}$$
$$\qquad \overline{1\frac{13}{36}}$$

- First, rewrite the problem with like denominators (LCD for 9 and 4 is 36).
- $\frac{1}{9}$ becomes $\frac{4}{36}$
- $\frac{3}{4}$ becomes $\frac{27}{36}$
- Now, realizing that you cannot subtract $\frac{4}{36} - \frac{27}{36}$ you must borrow.
- Borrow 1 from the 3 and consider it $\frac{36}{36}$.
- Add the $\frac{36}{36}$ that was borrowed to the $\frac{4}{36}$ already available ($\frac{36}{36} + \frac{4}{36} = \frac{40}{36}$).
- Now you are able to subtract. ($\frac{40}{36} - \frac{27}{36} = \frac{13}{36}$ and $2 - 1 = 1$ in the whole numbers.)
- Reduce if necessary.
- Final answer is $1\frac{13}{36}$.

Problems   Subtract the following pairs of fractions, and write the final answer in lowest terms.

1) $\dfrac{5}{8}$
     $-\dfrac{4}{8}$

2) $\dfrac{14}{15}$
     $-\dfrac{4}{6}$

3) $\dfrac{12}{14}$
     $-\dfrac{7}{10}$

4) $\dfrac{11}{12}$
     $-\dfrac{5}{12}$

5) $\dfrac{11}{12}$
     $-\dfrac{8}{15}$

6) $\dfrac{8}{10}$
     $-\dfrac{3}{4}$

7) $\dfrac{3}{10}$
     $-\dfrac{1}{10}$

8) $\dfrac{13}{14}$
     $-\dfrac{4}{7}$

9) $\dfrac{7}{12}$
     $-\dfrac{3}{8}$

10) $7\dfrac{6}{10}$
      $-5\dfrac{1}{3}$

11) $7\dfrac{3}{10}$
      $-4\dfrac{4}{5}$

12) $2\dfrac{8}{9}$
      $-2\dfrac{7}{12}$

13) $4\dfrac{7}{9}$
      $-1\dfrac{1}{3}$

14) $7\dfrac{4}{5}$
      $-\dfrac{5}{8}$

15) $16\dfrac{2}{5}$
      $-13\dfrac{7}{10}$

16)   Raina Morgan is remodeling her $1425\frac{1}{2}$ square foot salon. If she takes $115\frac{3}{4}$ square feet of space from her main salon to make a laundry room how much space will she have left?   _____

17)   Hannah Fredericks made a cleaning solution that is three parts water to one part Chlora-Mine. If she uses a one cup measure for each part, how much total solution will she have? Then, if she uses $\frac{1}{8}$ cup of it, how much will she have left?   _____

18)   Jayne Griffiths has three cases of cotton neck wrap in her salon. Each case divides easily into 100 strips. Everytime she uses one strip, she has used $\frac{1}{100}$ of a case (1 part out of 100 possible). In the first week, Jayne used 66 strips. Express 66 strips as a fraction and subtract it from the three cases she started with to determine how much cotton is left.   _____

19)   Craig completed his manager's training immediately after he finished his regular cosmetology training. He took $1015\frac{1}{2}$ hours of regular training and $125\frac{3}{4}$ hours of manager's training. How much longer did his regular training take than his manager's training?   _____

20)   Tammy Ocala works 40 hours a week. This week she took $2\frac{2}{3}$ hours off for a doctor's appointment. How many hours did she work this week?   _____

Multiplication

To multiply fractions, it is the same as trying to find a certain part of a part. For example what is $\frac{1}{2}$ of $\frac{3}{4}$? This is a multiplication problem. To understand what $\frac{1}{2}$ of $\frac{3}{4}$ really is, let's look at figure 4-3.

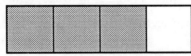

FIGURE 4-3 (From Dunlap/*MATHEMATICS FOR HEALTH OCCUPATIONS*, Copyright 1991 by Delmar Publishers Inc.)

At first $\frac{3}{4}$ of the diagram was filled in (indicated by first three boxes). Then, in finding $\frac{1}{2}$ of that, half of each box was shaded in. Half of $\frac{3}{4}$ is represented by the shaded part. This is really equivalent to 3 parts out of 8 possible (or $\frac{3}{8}$) as shown by figure 4–4.

FIGURE 4–4 (From Dunlap/*MATHEMATICS FOR HEALTH OCCUPATIONS,*
Copyright 1991 by Delmar Publishers Inc.)

Three shaded areas out of eight possible is $\frac{3}{8}$.

When you multiply fractions it is not necessary to have like denominators. It is important however that all mixed numbers are changed to improper fractions first before multiplying.

Then you multiply the numerators together and write the result on top and multiply the denominators together and write the result on the bottom. Then reduce to the lowest terms if necessary.

$$\frac{1}{2} \times \frac{3}{4} = \frac{3}{8} \qquad — \qquad \begin{array}{l} 1 \times 3 = 3 \\ 2 \times 4 = 8 \end{array}$$

Example 1: Multiply 4/5 × 7/8

$$\frac{4}{5} \times \frac{7}{8} = \frac{28}{40} \qquad — \qquad \begin{array}{l} 4 \times 7 = 28 \\ 5 \times 8 = 40 \end{array}$$

This can be reduced since 4 divides into 28 and 40 evenly.

$$\frac{28}{40} \div \frac{4}{4} = \frac{7}{10} \qquad \bullet \text{ The final answer is } \frac{7}{10}.$$

It is also possible to reduce before you multiply. If either numerator and either denominator can be divided evenly by some number, that can be done first before multiplication. In example 1, the 4 in $\frac{4}{5}$ (a numerator) and the 8 in $\frac{7}{8}$ (a denominator) both can be divided evenly by 4. Do this first and see what the result will be:

$$\overset{1}{\cancel{\frac{4}{5}}} \times \frac{7}{\underset{2}{\cancel{8}}} = \frac{7}{10} \qquad \bullet \text{ You still get } \frac{7}{10} \text{ as your final answer.}$$

Example 2: Multiply 1 3/4 × 2 5/6

$$1\frac{3}{4} \times 2\frac{5}{6} =$$ • You must change all mixed numbers to improper fractions first.

$$\frac{7}{4} \times \frac{17}{6} =$$ • Now you can multiply the numerators and the denominators or reduce first if possible.

$$\frac{7}{4} \times \frac{17}{6} = \frac{119}{24}$$ • This must then be reduced to lowest terms (that is, back to a mixed number in lowest terms).

• The final answer is $4\frac{23}{24}$.

$$\begin{array}{r} 4 \\ 24\overline{)119} \\ -\ 96 \\ \hline 23 \end{array}$$

Example 3:   Multiply 3 1/2 x 4

$$3\frac{1}{2} \times 4 =$$
- You must change all mixed numbers to improper fractions first (the number 4 becomes 4 over 1).

$$\frac{7}{2} \times \frac{4}{1} =$$
- Now you can multiply the numerators and the denominators or reduce first if possible.

$$\frac{7}{\cancel{2}} \times \frac{\cancel{4}^{2}}{1} = \frac{14}{1}$$
- Which equals 14 whole units.

Problems   Multiply the following pairs of fractions or mixed numbers and reduce to lowest terms.

1) $1\frac{2}{3} \times \frac{5}{6}$ _____ 	11) $5\frac{2}{5} \times \frac{7}{10}$ _____

2) $\frac{2}{5} \times \frac{7}{8}$ _____ 	12) $2\frac{1}{4} \times 4\frac{5}{6}$ _____

3) $\frac{7}{10} \times \frac{3}{4}$ _____ 	13) $7\frac{2}{3} \times 3\frac{3}{7}$ _____

4) $\frac{1}{2} \times \frac{4}{5}$ _____ 	14) $3\frac{1}{2} \times 3\frac{1}{2}$ _____

5) $1\frac{4}{9} \times \frac{3}{4}$ _____ 	15) $5 \times 3\frac{1}{4}$ _____

6) $3\frac{1}{4} \times 2\frac{8}{9}$ _____ 	16) $3\frac{1}{6} \times 7$ _____

7) $4\frac{1}{6} \times \frac{3}{8}$ _____ 	17) $4\frac{2}{5} \times 6\frac{1}{8}$ _____

8) $3\frac{3}{4} \times \frac{4}{5}$ _____ 	18) $3\frac{1}{3} \times 5\frac{4}{5}$ _____

9) $1\frac{4}{7} \times \frac{7}{8}$ _____ 	19) $1\frac{1}{2} \times 6$ _____

10) $4\frac{1}{5} \times 6\frac{5}{8}$ _____ 	20) $3\frac{4}{5} \times 7\frac{1}{2}$ _____

21) Janice co-owns Glamour Shop with three other women. They each purchase $\frac{1}{4}$ of the shop's supplies. When a recent order came in, Janice needed to determine how much of the order was actually hers. Find $\frac{1}{4}$ of the following amounts. _____

   15 $\frac{3}{4}$ cases of permanent wave solution

   18 $\frac{1}{2}$ cases of end wraps

   13 $\frac{2}{3}$ cases of brushes

   7 $\frac{1}{8}$ cases of combs

   12 $\frac{1}{5}$ cases of cleaning solution

22) Lauren wants to rearrange her shop. Will three 35$\frac{3}{4}$" styling stations fit side by side on a 7' wall? _____

23) Joy decides to double her order from last month with the local beauty supply store. What will her new order be if she ordered the following last month? _____

   3 capes for haircutting

   2 $\frac{1}{2}$ cases of hair color solution

   3 $\frac{2}{3}$ cases of cotton

   4 $\frac{5}{8}$ cases of permanent wave solution

24) Gretchen Maybree needs to find the dimensions of her salon so that she can order new flooring. Her old flooring comes in squares that are 8$\frac{1}{8}$" wide. To find the size of the room she can multiply the number of tiles

by the length of each tile. If there are $63\frac{1}{2}$ tiles from the front of her salon to the back and 48 from side to side, what are the dimensions of her shop—front to back? Side to side? _____

25) Kristianne Quinn owns Quinn's Cuts. She runs a regular ad in the Town Squire News to advertise her shop. An ad $3\frac{1}{2}$" wide (the width of one column) costs \$12.50 ($12\frac{1}{2}$ dollars) per inch in length. Using fractions, determine the cost of an ad that is $4\frac{1}{4}$" long. Show your work. _____

Division

To divide fractions it is the same as trying to find out what larger number your fraction is a part of. For example, what is $\frac{3}{4}$ half of? This is a division problem. To understand what $\frac{3}{4} \div \frac{1}{2}$ really is, let's look at the figure 4–5.

FIGURE 4–5 (From Dunlap/*MATHEMATICS FOR HEALTH OCCUPATIONS,*
Copyright 1991 by Delmar Publishers Inc.)

Three fourths of the diagram is shaded in (indicated by the first three boxes). Then, to find out what larger number this is half of, we must double the picture to create 2 sets of three fourths. Then we will know that our original set of three fourths was only half of that (1 set out of 2 sets drawn), figure 4–6.

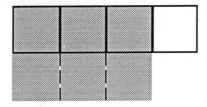

FIGURE 4–6 (From Dunlap/*MATHEMATICS FOR HEALTH OCCUPATIONS,*
Copyright 1991 by Delmar Publishers Inc.)

The larger number that $\frac{3}{4}$ is half of is six-fourths. Six shaded areas out of four possible, $\frac{6}{4}$.
$\frac{3}{4} \div \frac{1}{2} = \frac{6}{4}$

To better understand division of fractions, you must realize that you are "undoing" multiplication (just as division is the opposite of multiplication in whole numbers). When we needed to know what larger number $\frac{3}{4}$ was half of we had to double $\frac{3}{4}$. The opposite of finding a half is to double.

To divide fractions, you must first change all mixed numbers to improper fractions (as in multiplication). Then, invert the second fraction...that is, turn it upside down ($\frac{1}{2}$ becomes $\frac{2}{1}$). Be sure to always invert the **second** fraction not the first one. Once this has been done you can multiply the two fractions together.

Let's consider our example of $\frac{3}{4} \div \frac{1}{2}$.

$$\frac{3}{4} \div \frac{1}{2} = \qquad \text{becomes} \qquad \frac{3}{4} \times \frac{2}{1} = \frac{6}{4}$$

This answer is proof of our picture above and is the correct answer. It must now be reduced to lowest terms (that is, changed to a mixed number and then reduced). $\frac{6}{4} = 1\frac{2}{4} = 1\frac{1}{2}$

Example 1: $1\frac{1}{2} \div 1\frac{1}{5} =$

$1\frac{1}{2} \div 1\frac{1}{5} =$

$\frac{3}{2} \div \frac{6}{5} =$

$\frac{\cancel{3}^{1}}{2} \times \frac{5}{\cancel{6}_{2}} = \frac{5}{4}$

- First, change the mixed numbers to improper fractions.
- Now invert (turn over) the second fraction and multiply (reduce first if possible).
- $1 \times 5 = 5$
- $2 \times 2 = 4$

Reduce to lowest terms by changing back to a mixed number. $\frac{5}{4}$ becomes $1\frac{1}{4}$. The final answer is $1\frac{1}{4}$.

REMEMBER: Once you have inverted the second fraction, the problem proceeds just like a fraction multiplication problem.

Problems   Divide the following pairs of fractions or mixed numbers and reduce to lowest terms.

1) $\frac{7}{8} \div \frac{3}{8}$ _____

2) $1\frac{2}{7} \div 1\frac{1}{2}$ _____

3) $2\frac{1}{2} \div 1\frac{2}{8}$ _____

4) $2\frac{1}{3} \div 1\frac{3}{4}$ _____

5) $1\frac{4}{11} \div 5$ (same as 5/1) _____

6) $\frac{6}{7} \div 7$ _____

7) $1\frac{1}{3} \div \frac{11}{16}$ _____

8) $\frac{9}{10} \div \frac{2}{5}$ _____

9) $\frac{7}{9} \div \frac{7}{9}$ _____

10) $5 \div \frac{3}{5}$ _____

11) $5\frac{1}{3} \div \frac{2}{3}$ _____

12) $1\frac{3}{5} \div \frac{7}{10}$ _____

13) $1\frac{5}{7} \div \frac{3}{7}$ _____

14) $3\frac{1}{3} \div \frac{5}{6}$ _____

15) $2\frac{3}{4} \div \frac{1}{4}$ _____

16) Paula VanDell knows that she is one-third of the way through the schooling that is required to be a cosmetologist. She has completed $145\frac{1}{4}$ hours. How many total hours will be required of her? _____

17) Nora Sanders has two-fifths of the money required for a down payment on a new salon. She has saved $1400 so far. What is the total down payment that she is required to save? _____

18) Kyla Blair runs a regular ad in the Sweetwater Journal. She usually pays $45.75 ($45\frac{3}{4}$ dollars) for a $\frac{1}{8}$ page ad. How much would a full page ad cost? _____

19) Jennifer Dentalman is usually busy five-eighths of her work day. She has a regular client list of 75 people. How many clients would she need to have to run a full schedule? _____

20) Maryanne Walters owns a beauty salon with 6 operators. Only 4 of them work at a time. If the shop makes $496 a day, how much could they make if everyone worked? _____

Mixed Operations

Problems   Complete the following problems, using all necessary fraction operations.

1) Sally Reese used $3\frac{1}{2}$ oz. of disinfectant solution to clean her styling station after each client. On a day when she has 14 clients how many ounces does she use altogether?   _____

2) Carla Crouse kept inventory of the beauty supplies at Hanover House of Style. The supplies are kept in three separate dispensaries throughout the shop. In the first dispensary she found $2\frac{1}{4}$ cases of perm solution, 6 cases of tint solution, $3\frac{1}{8}$ bottles of cold cream, and $4\frac{1}{2}$ bottles of nail polish. In the second closet she found $1\frac{1}{8}$ cases of perm solution, $3\frac{1}{2}$ cases of tint solution, $4\frac{1}{4}$ bottles of cold cream, and 5 bottles of nail polish. In the third closet she found $5\frac{1}{8}$ cases of perm solution, $3\frac{1}{8}$ cases of tint solution, $4\frac{1}{16}$ bottles of cold cream, and $3\frac{1}{4}$ bottles of nail polish. Answer the following in fractions of a case.

a. How much perm solution does she have altogether?   _____

b. How much tint solution does she have altogether?   _____

c. How much cold cream does she have altogether?   _____

d. How much nail polish does she have altogether?   _____

3) After Carla takes inventory she must do whatever ordering is needed. If her goal is to keep at least 2 dozen cases (altogether) of each solution in stock and 1 dozen bottles of cold cream and nail polish in stock, how much of each item does she need? (Leave in fractional amounts even though she would order full bottles or cases.)

a. Perm solution?   _____

b. Tint solution?   _____

c. Cold cream?   _____

d. Nail polish?   _____

4) Karen Smith wants to rearrange the styling room of her salon. Each styling station is $35\frac{3}{4}$" wide and she would like to put as many stations as possible on one wall. How many stations will fit on a 13' wall? How much extra space would there be between the styling stations? (Draw a picture of the styling stations placed on the wall and show the distance between them.)   _____

5) Yvonne Farington pays part of the shipping cost of her beauty supply order when it exceeds 40 lbs total. The cost of shipping is $3.50 ($3\frac{1}{2}$ dollars) a pound for anything over 40 lbs. What is she required to pay if the items she orders weigh the following: $15\frac{5}{8}$ lb, $3\frac{3}{4}$ lb, $10\frac{7}{16}$ lb, $4\frac{1}{2}$ lb, $4\frac{1}{8}$ lb, $12\frac{5}{8}$ lb, and $4\frac{5}{16}$ lb.   _____

6) George is remodeling his barber shop. The equipment supply company is willing to take his old items for a trade-in and will take $\frac{1}{4}$ off of the price of the new items he chooses. His new items total $1512. How much will he actually pay after they take $\frac{1}{4}$ off?   _____

7) Kevin Harrigan had $55\frac{1}{4}$ boxes of end wraps in inventory a month ago. Now he has $27\frac{5}{8}$ boxes left. How many boxes have been used?   _____

8) Janice Wagner gets paid time and a half for each hour of overtime. This is the same as getting paid for the hours overtime that she works plus half as many more (or $1\frac{1}{2}$ times the overtime hours). How many overtime hours will she get credit for working if she works $5\frac{1}{4}$ hours overtime?   _____

9) Nora Wilson has 3 uniforms for her new job. When she interviewed for the job, they said that she must have 5 different uniforms that she could wear. What fraction of the uniforms needed does she have?   _____

10) Bob Nolton has $\frac{1}{2}$ of his required hours to be a manager. He has completed $74\frac{1}{2}$ hours so far. How many does he need altogether?   _____

Chapter 5

Combined Operations

It is necessary at times to convert a number to a different form to make it more meaningful or useful in mathematical operations. The various forms covered in this section—decimal, fraction, and percent—are all interchangeable. We will learn how to convert correctly from one form to another to obtain an equality which can be further used to interpret or solve a problem.

Defining a Percent

The word **percent** means "per one hundred" or "parts of each hundred." The percent symbol after 23% means that 23 parts out of 100 possible are represented.

You might say you've spent 25% more than you planned or you received a 5% raise. This is a comparison of the part (amount spent or amount of increase) to the whole amount (amount budgeted or amount currently earning).

Often standards are set on a 100 point scale. For example grading is often figured based on 100 points. Sales, discounts, and statistics are often based on the percentage system as well.

Percent to Decimal

Changing a percent to a decimal is a simple process when you understand what a percent is. Remember that a percent is defined as a certain number of parts out of 100 possible. That means that a percent is the same as a hundredth. In our number system, the hundredths place is two to the right of the decimal. Let's look at an example. 42% is 42 out of a 100 or 42 hundredths. Forty-two hundredths is written as .42 (ending in the hundredths place—two to the right of the decimal). Therefore 42% = .42

A standard rule for changing a percent to a decimal is to move the decimal two places to the left. This is also the same as the result you would get if you divide the number in the percent expression by 100. 42 ÷ 100 = .42 (moved two to the left).

Example 1: Change 12.5% to a decimal.

Move the decimal two places to the left and remove the percent sign.

$$12.5\% = .125$$

Example 2: Change 7% to a decimal.

Move the decimal two places to the left and remove the percent sign.

Remember: In a whole number, the decimal is understood to be at the right of the number.

$$7.\% = .07$$

Example 3: Change 125% to a decimal.

Move the decimal two places to the left and remove the percent sign.

$$125\% = 1.25$$

Problems   Change the following percents to decimals.

1)	55% _____	11)	125.5% _____	21)	71% _____
2)	7% _____	12)	11% _____	22)	200% _____
3)	65% _____	13)	10% _____	23)	5% _____
4)	60% _____	14)	4.25% _____	24)	68.7% _____
5)	100% _____	15)	8.1% _____	25)	45% _____
6)	78.33% _____	16)	873% _____	26)	13% _____
7)	49% _____	17)	372.2% _____	27)	1% _____
8)	.05% _____	18)	35.1% _____	28)	99% _____
9)	74% _____	19)	.361% _____	29)	3.6% _____
10)	13.5% _____	20)	15% _____	30)	68.5% _____

31) Randi gets a twenty-seven and a half percent commission where she works. Write this as a percent and then as a decimal. _____

32) Evelyn receives a two percent discount if she pays her supply bill within 15 days. Write this as a decimal. _____

33) Olivia Wagner scored a 79% on her recent test. Write this as a decimal. _____

34) Marsha receives a 41% commission where she works. Write this as a decimal. _____

35) Scott pays 18.75% interest on his credit card. Write this as a decimal. _____

Decimal to Percent

Changing a decimal to a percent is the reverse process of changing a percent to a decimal. This can be accomplished by moving the decimal two places to the right. It is necessary to write a % sign after the number once the decimal placement has been changed.

Example 1: Change .475 to a percent.

Move the decimal two places to the right and add a % sign.

$$.475 = 47.5\%$$

Example 2: Change 3 to a percent.

Move the decimal two places to the right and add a % sign.

$$3. = 300\%$$

Example 3: Change .4 to a percent.

Move the decimal two places to the right and add a % sign.

$$.4 = 40\%$$

Problems   Change the following decimals to a percent.

1) .578 _____	11) .007 _____	21) 64 _____
2) 1.6 _____	12) .26 _____	22) .36 _____
3) .7314 _____	13) 5.3 _____	23) .0006 _____
4) .71 _____	14) .371 _____	24) .70 _____
5) 4 _____	15) 7.22 _____	25) .001 _____
6) .722 _____	16) 10 _____	26) .03 _____
7) .111 _____	17) 3.33 _____	27) .005 _____
8) 1 _____	18) .4 _____	28) .732 _____
9) .6 _____	19) .88 _____	29) 13.5 _____
10) .1 _____	20) .14 _____	30) 1.1 _____

31)   Connie pays .045 times the amount of any purchase for state sales tax. What is her state sales tax rate as a percent?   _____

32)   Yvonne has two and a half times more customers that she used to have. What is her percent of increase?   _____

33)   Earl is seven tenths of the way through his schooling. Write this first as a decimal and then as a percent.   _____

34)   Jill pays .025 times the amount of any purchase when she uses her credit card and fails to pay it off at the end of the month. What is the percent of interest that she pays monthly? What is the yearly rate of interest (multiply by 12)?   _____

35)   Kelli pays her employees .45 times their sales as a commission. What is the rate of commission she pays?   _____

Decimal to Fraction

To change a decimal to a fraction, you must determine what place value the decimal is holding. For example .335 is holding the thousandths place (3 to the right of the decimal). Once you know its place value the fraction is written with that place value as the denominator. In the case of .335, your fraction becomes $\frac{335}{1000}$ (335 parts out of 1000 possible). Then, this must be reduced if possible.

$$.335 = \frac{335}{1000} \div \frac{5}{5} = \frac{67}{200}$$

The final answer is $\frac{67}{200}$.

Occasionally the decimal will also have a whole number to the left of the decimal point. When this occurs leave that whole number out of the changing process and then write it back in when you have reduced the fraction. For example, in 1.1 you have the whole number 1 and 1 tenth. The decimal part (.1) becomes $\frac{1}{10}$. Since this is lowest terms, rejoin the whole number 1 with the fraction for a final answer of $1\frac{1}{10}$.

Example 1:   Change .885 to a fraction.

Determine the place value being held and rewrite as a fraction.

$$.885 = \frac{885}{1000} \div \frac{5}{5} = \frac{177}{200}$$

The final answer is $\frac{177}{200}$.

Example 2:   Change 1.05 to a fraction.

1. Determine the place value being held and rewrite as a fraction. (The decimal part only)

$$.05 = \frac{5}{100} \div \frac{5}{5} = \frac{1}{20}$$

2. Rejoin the whole number with the fraction.

3. The final answer is $1\frac{1}{20}$.

Problems   Change the following decimals to fractions.

1) 4.56 _____	11) 3.7 _____	21) .007 _____
2) .8 _____	12) .015 _____	22) 1.6 _____
3) 25.1 _____	13) 7.50 _____	23) .42 _____
4) .62 _____	14) 71.85 _____	24) .71 _____
5) .154 _____	15) .26 _____	25) .88 _____
6) 1.68 _____	16) .25 _____	26) .027 _____
7) .080 _____	17) .16 _____	27) .22 _____
8) .789 _____	18) .35 _____	28) .64 _____
9) .3 _____	19) .04 _____	29) .025 _____
10) 3.5 _____	20) .75 _____	30) .002 _____

31) Carole works with a hand soap that is labeled .98 in purity. How many parts out of 100 would be considered *impure*? _____

32) Deanna received a .78 on a recent test. Rewrite this as a fraction to determine how many she got correct out of 50. _____

33) Joanne is assessed .035 of the value of her property in property taxes. Express this as a fraction. _____

34) Crystal has a .9875 average in her cosmetology classes. Express this as a fraction. _____

35) Clayton received a .95 approval rating in a contest. If there were twenty judges, how many voted for him? _____

Fraction to Decimal

Changing a fraction to a decimal requires division. The numerator of the fraction becomes the dividend and the denominator of the fraction becomes the divisor.

Example 1:   Change $\frac{3}{5}$ to a decimal.

$$
\begin{array}{r}
.6 \\
5\,\overline{)\,3.0} \\
-3\,0 \\
\hline
0
\end{array}
$$

The remainder is zero; this is a terminating decimal.

Final answer: $\frac{3}{5} = .6$

Example 2:   Change $\frac{1}{8}$ to a decimal.

$$
\begin{array}{r}
.125 \\
8\,\overline{)\,1.000} \\
-\ 8 \\
\hline
20 \\
-16 \\
\hline
40 \\
-40 \\
\hline
0
\end{array}
$$

The remainder is zero; this is a terminating decimal.

Final answer: $\frac{1}{8} = .125$

Some fractions will divide out evenly (meaning that division will have no remainder). These decimals are called **terminating** decimals because they eventually end. The previous two examples have been **terminating** decimals.

Other fractions will not divide out evenly. These decimals are called **repeating** decimals because they will eventually develop a pattern that repeats itself in the decimal. Some repeating decimals tend to repeat very early in the division and some do not. But in either case, since division will never come out evenly, there is a notation that can be used to express the answer obtained from division. When a number or group of numbers in your solution repeats, place a line over the number or group to indicate the repetition.

Example 3:   Change $\frac{1}{3}$ to a decimal.

$$
\begin{array}{r}
.333 \\
3\,\overline{)\,1.000} \\
-\ 9 \\
\hline
10 \\
-\ 9 \\
\hline
10 \\
-\ 9 \\
\hline
1
\end{array}
$$

- Use as many zero place holders as necessary.

- The remainder 1 will continue to show up no matter how long we divide; this is a repeating decimal.

Since the 3 in .333 is the only digit repeating, we need only write one 3 with a line over it.

Final answer: $\frac{1}{3} = .\overline{3}$

Example 4: Change $\frac{1}{22}$ to a decimal.

$$
\begin{array}{r}
.04545 \\
22 \overline{)\ 1.00000} \\
-\ \ 88 \\
\hline
120 \\
-\ 110 \\
\hline
100 \\
-\ \ 88 \\
\hline
120 \\
-\ 110 \\
\hline
10
\end{array}
$$

The remainder 10 will continue to show up no matter how long we divide; this is a repeating decimal. Since the number group 45 is the repeating part of the decimal we will put a line over both digits.

Final answer: $\frac{1}{22} = .0\overline{45}$

When working with a repeating decimal that does not repeat early in the division, it is sometimes more practical to round that number to a certain place value than it would be to complete the division. In this book, if you have not found a repeating pattern or a termination by the 100,000th place (5 places to the right of the decimal), round the answer to the nearest 10,000th place (4 places to the right of the decimal).

Example 5: Change $\frac{3}{26}$ to a decimal.

$$
\begin{array}{r}
.11538 \\
26 \overline{)\ 3.00000} \\
-\ 26 \\
\hline
40 \\
-\ 26 \\
\hline
140 \\
-\ 130 \\
\hline
100 \\
-\ 78 \\
\hline
220 \\
-\ 208 \\
\hline
12
\end{array}
$$

Final answer: .11538 rounds to .1154

When the fraction is a mixed number, leave the whole number out of the changing process and then write it back in when you have solved the division and are writing the final answer.

Problems   Change the following fractions to decimals. If division does not terminate or repeat before 100,000ths place, round the answers to the nearest 10,000ths place.

1) $\frac{4}{5}$ _____		6) $\frac{1}{16}$ _____		11) $\frac{7}{8}$ _____	
2) $\frac{5}{6}$ _____		7) $\frac{7}{9}$ _____		12) $\frac{3}{4}$ _____	
3) $\frac{1}{10}$ _____		8) $\frac{4}{8}$ _____		13) $1\frac{1}{2}$ _____	
4) $1\frac{5}{12}$ _____		9) $3\frac{1}{5}$ _____		14) $6\frac{1}{7}$ _____	
5) $4\frac{3}{10}$ _____		10) $5\frac{14}{15}$ _____		15) $\frac{19}{20}$ _____	

16) Roger got 17 problems correct out of 25. What is his grade as a decimal? _____

17) Carolyn received 6 of the 7 boxes that were to be shipped. Write a decimal that represents the part of the order that she has received. _____

18) Todd normally gets paid $55 a day for delivering beauty supplies for a local distributor. Today he had to take 1 hour off (out of an 8 hour day) to go to the doctor. What part of the day did he work (as a decimal)? How much should he be paid? _____

19) Becky Brant is required to take 1150 hours of training to apply for her state board license to practice cosmetology. She has completed 1035 hours so far. How many hours does she have yet to complete? Express that as a decimal. _____

20) Claire Connors scored 24 out of 25 on a recent test. What is her score as a decimal? _____

Percent to Fraction

There are two ways that a percent can be changed to a fraction. The first is to realize that a percent means a certain number of parts out of 100 possible. So 15% means 15 out of 100 or $\frac{15}{100}$. This only needs to be reduced. $(15\% = \frac{15}{100} = \frac{3}{20})$ This is by far the easiest way of changing a percent to a fraction and should be the first method that you try.

The second method is effective when the percent contains a decimal, like 14.5%. In this case it is best to change the percent to a decimal first (as learned in a previous section) and then change that decimal to a fraction. So to change 14.5% to a decimal, you must move the decimal point two places to the left and eliminate the % sign. (14.5% = .145) Next, realize that .145 is in the 1000ths place and rewrite the decimal as a fraction. $(.145 = \frac{145}{1000})$ This must then be reduced. $(.145 = \frac{145}{1000} = \frac{29}{200})$ The second method involves a few more steps, but it is the safest way to insure a correct answer when the original percent is written in a complicated way.

Example 1: Change 100% to a fraction.

100% means 100 parts out of 100 possible.

$$100\% = \frac{100}{100} = 1$$

Example 2: Change 5% to a fraction.

5% means 5 parts out of 100 possible.

$$5\% = \frac{5}{100} = \frac{1}{20}$$

Example 3: Change 16.64% to a fraction.

1. Since this percent contains a decimal, use the second method (percent to decimal, then decimal to fraction.)

$$16.64\% = .1664$$

2. This is in the 10,000ths place:

$$.1664 = \frac{1,664}{10,000} = \frac{104}{625}$$

3. Numerator and denominator were divided by 16.

Example 4: Change 450% to a fraction.

450% means 450 parts out of 100 possible.

$$450\% = \frac{450}{100} = \frac{9}{2} = 4\frac{1}{2}$$

This must be written as a mixed number in lowest terms.

Problems Change the following percents to decimals.

1) 50% _____	11) 42.5% _____	21) 6% _____
2) 102% _____	12) 96% _____	22) 10% _____
3) 11.5% _____	13) 14% _____	23) 7.25% _____
4) 33% _____	14) 70% _____	24) 110% _____
5) 4% _____	15) 65% _____	25) 12% _____
6) 47.2% _____	16) 51.25% _____	26) 11% _____
7) 8% _____	17) 52% _____	27) .25% _____
8) 1.6% _____	18) 1% _____	28) 32% _____
9) 116% _____	19) 26.75% _____	29) 38% _____
10) 3% _____	20) 162% _____	30) 18% _____

31) Justin completed 85% of the perms that he had scheduled for the week. Express this percent as a fraction. Out of 20 perms, how many has he completed? _____

32) Teresa McGuire earned a 94% on her final state board examination in cosmetology. How many problems did she do correctly out of 50? _____

33) Janna usually has 60% of her employees working in her beauty shop at any given time. If she has five employees, how many does she usually schedule at one time? _____

34) LaShanda receives 45% commission for her work at Value Salon. Express this as a fraction. _____

35) Regina pays 3.5% state income tax. Express this as a fraction. _____

Fraction to Percent

To change a fraction to a percent it is first necessary to change the fraction to a decimal by division (as learned in a previous section). Then change that decimal to a percent by moving the decimal two places to the right and adding a % sign.

Example 1: Change $\frac{3}{5}$ to a percent to determine your score on a quiz.

1. Change $\frac{3}{5}$ to a decimal by division.

```
     .6
 5 ) 3.0
   - 3 0
       0
```

2. Change that decimal to a percent by moving the decimal two places to the right.

$$\frac{3}{5} = .6 = 60\% \text{ (add a zero place holder)}$$

Example 2:   Change $1\frac{7}{8}$ to a percent.

1. Change $\frac{7}{8}$ to a percent.

$$\begin{array}{r} .875 \\ 8 \overline{)\ 7.000} \\ -\ 6\,4 \\ \hline 60 \\ -\ 56 \\ \hline 40 \\ -\ 40 \\ \hline 0 \end{array}$$

- Remember the whole number 1 which has been set aside for now.

2. Change that decimal to a percent by moving the decimal two places to the right.

$$1\frac{7}{8} = 1.875 = 187.5\%$$

Example 3:   Change $\frac{1}{3}$ to a percent.

1. Change $\frac{1}{3}$ to a decimal by division.

$$\begin{array}{r} .33\ldots \\ 3 \overline{)\ 1.00} \\ -\ 9 \\ \hline 10 \\ -\ 9 \\ \hline 1 \end{array}$$

This is a repeating decimal; it will need to be rounded to a certain place value.

$$\frac{1}{3} = .\overline{3}$$

2. Change that decimal to a percent by moving the decimal two places to the right. Write this as a 5-digit decimal for all problems in this book and then round to a 4-digit number.

3. $\frac{1}{3} = .33333$ rounds to $.333 = 33.33\%$

Problems   Change the following fractions to percents.

1) $\frac{4}{7}$ _____

2) $\frac{5}{12}$ _____

3) $\frac{1}{2}$ _____

4) $\frac{2}{3}$ _____

5) $\frac{1}{9}$ _____

6) $\frac{3}{8}$ _____

7) $1\frac{4}{5}$ _____

8) $\frac{2}{5}$ _____

9) $\frac{1}{4}$ _____

10) $1\frac{1}{10}$ _____

11) $1\frac{3}{4}$ _____

12) $\frac{11}{12}$ _____

13) $\frac{1}{8}$ _____

14) $\frac{6}{10}$ _____

15) $\frac{13}{14}$ _____

16) Kelly got 7 problems correct out of 12. Write her score as a percent.   _____

17) Out of the 45 appointment times available, Donna schedules 32 regular customers each week. What percentage of her time is spent with regular customers? What percentage is spent with non-frequent or new customers?   _____

18) Michelle has 7 different perms available through her local supply store. She has only tried four of these on her customers. What percentage of the perms has she tried?   _____

19) Tracy works 2 days out of the 6 that the New You Shop is open. What percentage of the time is she there?   _____

20) Patti can finish her manager's training in 45 hours. If the total time required is 120 hours, what percentage does she have left?   _____

Percent — Base

To find a certain part of a whole or to find what percent of the whole is being represented or to find out what the whole number is to which you are comparing, you can work a percent-base problem. The percent represents the part you are comparing and the base is the whole to which you are comparing.

In a percent-base problem, there are three parts—the percent, the base and the part (or percentage).

$$16 \quad \times \quad .25 \quad = \quad 4$$

16 is the base	.25 is the percent	4 is the part
(whole)	(changed to a decimal)	(percentage)

This problem indicates that 25% (.25) of 16 is 4. Multiplication is used in this problem because of the word "of" and an equal sign replaces the word "is." Setting up the problem with the multiplication and equal signs is an important part of being able to solve it.

It will be necessary to solve a percent-base problem for each of the three possible answers. You might be asked: What is 15% of 200? Forty is 20% of what number? What percent of 80 is 24? Noticing the words "of" and "is" will help is setting up the problem and solving it. The word "what" indicates the missing answer. If the unknown answer **is not** alone on the left or right side of the equal sign, you must divide to find the solution. If the unknown answer **is** alone on the left or right side of the equal sign, you must multiply to find the solution.

Example 1: What is 15% of 200?

1. Put the problem into symbols and numbers.

    "what" = 15% × 200

2. Change the percent to decimal and solve.

    "what" = .15 × 200

3. Decide whether to multiply or divide. (Multiply because the unknown part is alone on the left side of the equals sign.)

$$\begin{array}{r} 200 \\ \times\ .15 \\ \hline 1000 \\ 200\ \ \\ \hline 30.00 \end{array}$$

4. 30 is 15% of 200

Example 2: Forty is 20% of what number?

1. Put the problem into symbols and numbers.

    40 = 20% × "what"

2. Change the percent to decimal and solve.

    40 = .20 × "what"

3. Decide whether to multiply or divide. (Divide because the unknown part is not alone.)

$$\begin{array}{r} 200. \\ .20\overline{)40.00} \\ -\underline{20} \\ 00 \end{array}$$

4. 40 is 20% of 200

Example 3: What percent of 80 is 24?

1. Put the problem into symbols and numbers.

"what %" × 80 = 24

2. Change the percent to decimal and solve. (We are looking for the percent; we can't change it now but we must once we find it.)

3. Decide whether to multiply or divide. (Divide because the unknown part is not alone.)

$$\begin{array}{r} .3 \\ 80\overline{)24.0} \\ -\underline{24\ 0} \\ 0 \end{array}$$

4. Change .3 to a percent (.3 = 30%)

5. 30% of 80 is 24

Problems Complete the following percent-base problems, finding the missing answer by multiplication or division.

1) What is 18% of 50? _____

2) 18 is 300% of what number? _____

3) 50% of 16 is what? _____

4) 54 is 90% of what number? _____

5) What percent of 70 is 28? _____

6) What is 80% of 20? _____

7) What is 24% of 40? _____

8) What percent of 220 is 11? _____

9) 45 is 30% of what number? _____

10) 93 is what percent of 93? _____

11) What percent of 40 is 14? _____

12) What is 35% of 200? _____

13) What percent of 90 is 22.5? _____

14) What is 88% of 40? _____

15) 63 is 25% of what number? _____

16) 85% of 400 is what? _____

17) What percent of 100 is 47? _____

18) What is 18% of 250? _____

19) What is 55% of 220? _____

20) What is 325% of 44? _____

Mixed Operations

Problems Fill in the blanks by converting between percents, decimals, and fractions.

	FRACTION	DECIMAL	PERCENT
1)	$\frac{3}{4}$	_____	_____
2)	_____	.87	_____
3)	_____	_____	5.25%
4)	_____	.005	_____
5)	_____	_____	16.5%
6)	$1\frac{7}{8}$	_____	_____
7)	$\frac{3}{50}$	_____	_____
8)	_____	.124	_____
9)	_____	_____	312%
10)	$\frac{19}{20}$	_____	_____
11)	_____	4.5	_____
12)	_____	_____	2%
13)	$4\frac{1}{20}$	_____	_____
14)	_____	.0625	_____
15)	_____	_____	.04%
16)	_____	.5	_____
17)	$\frac{5}{16}$	_____	_____
18)	_____	_____	11.25%
19)	_____	.006	_____
20)	_____	_____	5%

Chapter 6

Ratios and Proportions

Defining A Ratio

A **ratio** is an expression of comparison between two numbers. A ratio is usually written as one number before another with a colon in between. A ratio may also be expressed as a fraction, a decimal, or a quotient (one number divided by another).

The relationship between 1 and 4 can be written as 1:4 (standard notation), $\frac{1}{4}$ (fraction), .25 (decimal found by $1 \div 4$), or $1 \div 4$ (as a quotient).

Problems   Express the following ratios in the different forms requested. Reduce to lowest terms when possible.

Ratio	Fraction	Decimal
1) 1:3	_____	_____
2) 2:5	_____	_____
3) 10:25	_____	_____
4) 2:15	_____	_____
5) 4:12	_____	_____
6) 1:8	_____	_____
7) 15:20	_____	_____
8) 85:100	_____	_____
9) 7:10	_____	_____
10) 5:9	_____	_____

Express the following ratios in these forms: standard, fraction, and quotient. (HINT: Change to fraction in lowest terms first)

11) .46 _____

12) .15 _____

13) .77 _____

14) .05 _____

15) 1.35 _____

Defining a Proportion

A **proportion** expresses the relationship between two ratios. It is written as two ratios with an equal sign between. For example 2:7 = 6:21. The four numbers in the proportion have special names. The two outer numbers, in this case 2 and 21, are called the **extremes**. The two inner numbers, 7 and 6, are called the **means**. In a **true** (equal) proportion, the product of the means should equal the product of the extremes.

$$2{:}7 \ = \ 6{:}21$$

Means	Extremes
$7 \times 6 = 42$	$2 \times 21 = 42$

42 equals 42, thus this is a true proportion

Problems   Determine whether the following proportions are true. Show your work.

1) 4:5 = 12:15 _____   11) 6:7 = 7:6 _____

2) 1:5 = 3:14 _____   12) 8:4 = 2:1 _____

3) 16:3 = 4:.75 _____   13) 12:8 = 3:2 _____

4) 56:70 = 84:105 _____   14) 5:7 = 10:13 _____

5) 12:14 = 7:6 _____   15) 20:30 = 2:3 _____

6) 5:8 = 15:24 _____   16) 14:16 = 8:7 _____

7) 4:7 = 6:9 _____   17) 10:18 = 5:9 _____

8) 16:12 = 4:3 _____   18) 5:10 = 4:8 _____

9) 3:9 = 14:42 _____   19) 6:9 = 8:18 _____

10) 5:2 = 4:1 _____   20) 16:15 = 4:5 _____

Solving Proportions

If you know that a proportion is true (that the ratios are equal), you can solve for a missing part. This is very useful in the cosmetology field because it helps you prepare various solutions and mixtures. For example if you know that a cleaning solution requires 5 parts water to 3 parts chemical, you can determine how to mix the solution.

$$5{:}3 = \text{c. water: 2 c. chemical}$$

Since this is a true proportion, the product of the means equals the product of the extremes.

$$\text{Means} = \text{Extremes}$$
$$5 \times 2 = 3 \times \text{c. water}$$
$$10 = 3 \times \text{c. water}$$

Dividing both sides by three will help you solve the problem for the amount of water you need.

$$\frac{10}{3} = \frac{3 \times \text{c. water}}{3}$$

$$3\tfrac{1}{3} = \text{c. water}$$

The 3 over 3 cancels (becomes the whole number 1); $\frac{10}{3}$ simplifies to $3\frac{1}{3}$.

Proportions do not always contain just whole numbers as the means and extremes. Occasionally, they may contain fractions, decimals, or more complicated expressions. These too can be solved for the unknown amount.

Example 1: Some cleaning solutions are prepared by the following formula: $\frac{1}{2}$ tablet per pint of warm water. Josie needs to prepare 3 pints of water. How many tablets are needed?

$$\frac{tablets}{pints} \qquad \frac{\frac{1}{2}}{1} = \frac{tablets}{3}$$

$$\begin{aligned} \text{Means} \quad \text{Extremes} \\ 1 \text{ tabs} = \tfrac{1}{2}\,(3) \\ \text{tabs} = 1\tfrac{1}{2} \end{aligned}$$

Josie needs $1\frac{1}{2}$ tablets

It is wise to check your answers when you have solved a proportion. You should be able to replace the answer you found back into the original proportion, multiply the means and extremes, and the result will be a true proportion. If it is not, re-check your work.

Problems Solve for x in the following proportions. Check your work.

1) 4:5 = 12:x _____   11) x:7 = 12:42 _____
2) 8:x = 28:7 _____   12) 9:10 = x:15 _____
3) 4.5:5 = x:10 _____   13) 16:20 = x:5 _____
4) 8:x = 12:6 _____   14) 2.5:10 = x:24 _____
5) 7:x = 21:24 _____   15) 6:9 = 10:x _____
6) 13:x = 52:4 _____   16) 3:4 = x:16 _____
7) 19:x = 38:40 _____   17) x:6 = 7:42 _____
8) x:8 = 8:4 _____   18) 6:15 = 3:x _____
9) 7:10 = x:3.5 _____   19) 4:5 = x:15 _____
10) 13:3 = 13:x _____   20) 4:8 = 8:x _____

21) Grace needs to prepare a facial solution that requires 6 parts cold cream to 1 part water. How much water does she need to add to 16 oz. of cold cream? _____

22) Shannon cleans her implements with a mixture of denatured alcohol and water. If the required formula is 5 parts alcohol to 2 parts water, how much water must she add to 8 oz. of alcohol? _____

23) Lisa cleans the dispensary floor with ammonia and water. The mixture calls for 4 parts water to 1 part ammonia. How much ammonia should she add to a gallon of water? (Use ounces; a gallon has 128 oz.) _____

24) Adrianne treats her hands to a mixture of witch hazel and water after giving a permanent. If she uses a combination of 2 parts water to 3 parts witch hazel, how much witch hazel will she use to make a *total* mixture of 40 oz? (Hint: Since the question asks about total, your proportion needs to be set up as parts of witch hazel to *total* parts.) _____

25) Colette makes a solution requiring 7 parts water to 1 part chemical. If she plans to use 8 oz of chemical, how much water will she need? _____

Chapter 7

Measurement

Conversion Facts

Volume, length, and mass are the three main types of measurement. The English system is the system most common in the United States. In cosmetology it is widely used to measure the length of hair, the width and diameter of rollers, and the volume of various products.

The most common volume measurements in the English system include the gallon, half gallon, quart, pint, cup, ounce, tablespoon, and teaspoon. The most commonly used length measurements are the mile, yard, foot, and inches. The mass measurements include pounds and ounces.

To understand the English system and use it it is important to know some basic facts about the relationship of one measurement to another. It is also helpful to have a standard set of abbreviations to work with.

Volume

Abbreviations:
gallon — gal.
half gallon — $\frac{1}{2}$ gal.
quart — qt.
pint — pt.
cup — c.
ounce — oz.
tablespoon — T, tbl., tbsp.
teaspoon — t, tsp.

Equivalent measures:
1 gallon = 2 half gallons = 4 quarts
$\frac{1}{2}$ gallon = 2 quarts
1 quart = 2 pints
1 pint = 2 cups
1 cup = 8 ounces
1 ounce = 2 tablespoons
1 tablespoon = 3 teaspoons

Length

Abbreviations:
mile — mi.
yard — yd.
foot — ft. or '
inch — in. or "

Equivalent measures:
1 mile = 1760 yards or 5280 feet
1 yard = 3 feet
1 foot = 12 inches

Mass

Abbreviations:
pound — lb. or #
ounce — oz.

Equivalent measures:
1 pound = 16 ounces

The English system of measurement has been developed randomly (**three** teaspoons in a tablespoon, **four** quarts in a gallon, **16** ounces in a pound). Therefore, when we want to convert from one measurement to another, there is no shortcut to understanding the relationship that the various measurements have with each other. We must multiply or divide by different numbers for each different conversion. These numbers are called **conversion numbers**.

To find the **conversion number**, we will first write all of the same type measurements (volume, mass, or length) in order from largest to smallest in a column.

Example 1:   1 quart = _____ounces
                    gallon
                    half gallon
                    quart
                    pint
                    cup
                    ounce
                    tablespoon
                    teaspoon

Then we will write the facts that we know about these measurements along the side in an abbreviated way.

1 quart = _____ounces

* gallon	(there is nothing above on list)
2 half gallon	(gallon from above = 2 half gal.)
2 quart	(half gal from above = 2 qt.)
2 pint	(quart from above = 2 pt.)
2 cup	(pint from above = 2 c.)
8 ounce	(cup from above = 8 oz.)
2 tablespoon	(ounce from above = 2 tbl.)
3 teaspoon	(tbl. from above = 3 tsp.)

Now we need to determine what two measurements concern us in the conversion problem we are doing. In our example, this is quart and ounce. So we must find these measurements on the list.

2 quart	(half gal from above = 2 qt)
2 pint	(quart from above = 2 pt)
2 cup	(pint from above = 2 c.)
8 ounce	(cup from above = 8 oz.)

It is important to ignore the top number in this new list because it is information about the half gallon from above. We need all of the numbers except the top one. (2, 2, and 8) Multiply these numbers together. ($2 \times 2 \times 8 = 32$) This is your conversion number.

Once you have found your conversion number, the following rules will help you to complete the conversion.

1. When converting from a large unit to a smaller one, multiply by the **conversion number**.
2. When converting from a small unit to a larger one, divide by the **conversion number**.

In our example, 1 quart = _____ ounces, we are converting from a larger unit (quart) to a smaller unit (ounce). (This is made obvious because we are going **down** the list that we wrote—largest to smallest). Since we are going from large to small, we should multiply. **One** quart $\times 32 = 32$ ounces. 1 quart = 32 ounces.

This system of abbreviation with numbers is just a device to help you remember the equivalent facts about measurement. Let's look again at the list with the numbers along the side.

Volume

*	gallon	(there is nothing above on list)
2	half gallon	(gallon from above = 2 half gal.)
2	quart	(half gal from above = 2 qt.)
2	pint	(quart from above = 2 pt.)
2	cup	(pint from above = 2 c.)
8	ounce	(cup from above = 8 oz.)
2	tablespoon	(ounce from above = 2 tbl.)
3	teaspoon	(tbl. from above = 3 tsp.)

There are seven numbers there in the complete list...2, 2, 2, 2, 8, 2, and 3. Think of these seven numbers as a telephone number 222-2823. This is easy to remember and will help you convert the volume measurements. For length, the list is much shorter and not too difficult to remember. And for mass, you need only remember the number 16 (16 ounces in a pound).

Length

*	mile	
1760	yard	(mile from above = 1760 yds.)
3	foot	(yard from above = 3 ft.)
12	inch	(foot from above = 12 in.)

Mass

*	pound	
16	ounce	(pound from above = 16 oz.)

Example 2:   3 c. = _____ tbl.

1) Write the volume list.

   * gallon
   2 half gallon
   2 quart
   2 pint
   2 cup
   8 ounce
   2 tablespoon
   3 teaspoon

2) Find the two measurements on the list (c., tbl.)

   2 cup
   8 ounce
   2 tablespoon

3) Ignore the top number, multiply the rest. ($8 \times 2 = 16$)

4) Going from large to small, so multiply. **3 c. × 16** = 48

5) Solution: 3 c. = 48 tbl.

Example 3:   3520 ft. = _____ mi.

1)   Write the length list.

$$\begin{array}{rl} * & \text{mile} \\ 1760 & \text{yard} \\ 3 & \text{foot} \\ 12 & \text{inch} \end{array}$$

2)   Find the two measurements on the list (ft., mi.)

$$\begin{array}{rl} * & \text{mile} \\ 1760 & \text{yard} \\ 3 & \text{foot} \end{array}$$

3)   Ignore the top number, multiply the rest. (The top number is the *...ignore it. $1760 \times 3 = 5280$)

4)   Going from small to large, so divide. You have the choice here of: $\frac{3520}{5280}$ a fraction to be reduced or division.

   $$\textbf{3520 ft.} \div \textbf{5280} = \frac{2}{3}$$

5)   Solution: 3520 ft. = $\frac{2}{3}$ mi.

Example 4:   How many ounces are in a gallon?

In this example, it is necessary to first restate the problem in the form "what we're given...what we're trying to find." This is a process of setting up your problem so that it is always in the form "what we're given = _____ what we're trying to find." In this example, we know we have **one** gallon but we do not know how many ounces.

1)   Rewrite as: 1 gallon = _____ ounces

2)   Write the volume list.

$$\begin{array}{rl} * & \text{gallon} \\ 2 & \text{half gallon} \\ 2 & \text{quart} \\ 2 & \text{pint} \\ 2 & \text{cup} \\ 8 & \text{ounce} \\ 2 & \text{tablespoon} \\ 3 & \text{teaspoon} \end{array}$$

3)   Find the two measurements on the list (gal., oz.)

$$\begin{array}{rl} * & \text{gallon} \\ 2 & \text{half gallon} \\ 2 & \text{quart} \\ 2 & \text{pint} \\ 2 & \text{cup} \\ 8 & \text{ounce} \end{array}$$

3)   Ignore the top number, multiply the rest. (Ignore the *... $2 \times 2 \times 2 \times 2 \times 8 = 128$)

4)   Going from large to small so multiply. **1** gal. $\times$ **128** = 128

5)   Solution: 1 gal. = 128 oz.

Volume Measurement

In converting volume measurements, you will always need the list of volume measurements in order from largest to smallest.

* gallon
2 half gallon
2 quart
2 pint
2 cup
8 ounce
2 tablespoon
3 teaspoon

Problems   Complete the following conversions.

1) 3 gallons = _____ quarts

2) 5 ounces = _____ teaspoons

3) 16 ounces = _____ cups

4) 1 half gallon = _____ pints

5) 12 quarts = _____ gallons

6) 18 teaspoons = _____ tablespoons

7) 4 ounces = _____ cups

8) $1\frac{1}{2}$ quarts = _____ ounces

9) 4 tablespoons = _____ ounces

10) 3 pints = _____ cups

11) 1 qt. = _____ c.

12) 3 pt. = _____ tbl.

13) 1 oz. = _____ c.

14) 3 t. = _____ tbl.

15) 4 gal. = _____ qt.

In #16–#20 be sure to restate the problem as shown in example 3.

16) How many gallons are in 16 pints?   _____

17) How many teaspoons are in 1 ounce?   _____

18) Does a gallon have 16 cups in it?   _____

19) How many quarts are in 64 ounces?   _____

20) A pint equals how many cups?   _____

Length Measurement

In converting length measurements, you will always need the list of length measurements in order from largest to smallest.

```
   *  mile
1760  yard
   3  foot
  12  inch
```

Problems   Complete the following conversions.

1) 3 miles = _____ yards
2) 18 feet = _____ yards
3) 48 inches = _____ feet
4) 1 mile = _____ feet
5) $2\frac{1}{2}$ feet = _____ inches
6) 5280 feet = _____ miles
7) 66 inches = _____ feet
8) 108 inches = _____ yards

9) 4 yards = _____ feet
10) 3 feet = _____ yards
11) 6 inches = _____ feet
12) 144 inches = _____ yards
13) 1 mile = _____ inches
14) $\frac{1}{4}$ mile = _____ yards
15) 8 feet = _____ inches

In #16–#20 be sure to restate the problem as shown in the examples.

16) How many feet are in a mile? _____
17) How many inches tall is a 6'2" man? (6 foot, 2 inch) _____
18) How long in inches is a 12' board? _____
19) How many yards are in 72 feet? _____
20) A half mile contains how many feet? _____

Mass Measurement

In converting mass measurements, you will always need the list of mass measurements in order from largest to smallest.

```
  *  pound
 16  ounce
```

Problems   Complete the following conversions.

1) 3 lb. = _____ oz.
2) $4\frac{1}{2}$ lb. = _____ oz.
3) 2 lb. 6 oz. = _____ oz.
4) 24 oz. = _____ lb.
5) 4.2 lb. = _____ oz.
6) 10 lb. = _____ oz.
7) 120 oz. = _____ lb.
8) 8 oz. = _____ lb.

9) 3 lb. 14 oz. = _____ oz.
10) $3\frac{1}{2}$ lb. = _____ oz.
11) 1 lb. = _____ oz.
12) 80 oz. = _____ lb.
13) 4 lb. 7 oz. = _____ oz.
14) 5.25 lb. = _____ oz.
15) 176 oz. = _____ lb.

In #16–#20 be sure to restate the problem as shown in the examples.

16) How many ounces are in a 4 lb. watermelon? _____

17) How many ounces does a 5 lb. 3 oz. baby weigh? _____

18) Three pounds equals how many ounces? _____

19) How many pounds are in 152 ounces? _____

20) How many pounds are in 24 ounces? _____

Reading a Ruler

Cosmetologists are often asked to cut off a certain length of hair. This can be done only when you are familiar with reading a ruler accurately and then approximating that length.

Most rulers measure to the nearest $\frac{1}{16}$". This means that each inch is divided into 16 equal sections. You can read a certain length on a ruler by determining how many **whole** inches are marked off and then what additional **part** of an inch is marked.

Example 1: Read the length marked on the ruler.

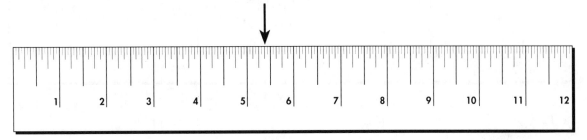

Figure 7-1

- There are 5 whole inches and 6 parts (out of 16) of another.
- This is $5\frac{6}{16}$" which reduces to $5\frac{3}{8}$"

Example 2: Read the length marked on the ruler.

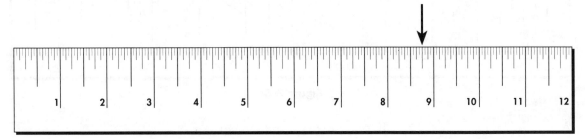

Figure 7-2

- There are 8 whole inches and 12 parts (out of 16) of another.
- This is $8\frac{12}{16}$" which reduces to $8\frac{3}{4}$"

Example 3: Mark the ruler at $7\frac{5}{8}$"

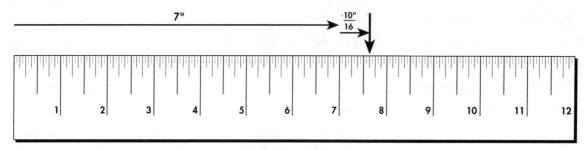

Figure 7-3

There are 7 whole inches, so the mark must be past 7. Then $\frac{5}{8}$" must be converted to 16ths $\frac{5}{8} = \frac{10}{16}$. Put the mark at the 10th line past the line 7.

Problems Mark the following ruler with the appropriate measurements. Draw an arrow to the point and label it with the letter of the problem.

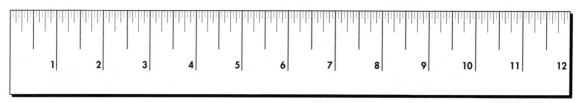

Figure 7-4

A — $5\frac{1}{4}$" _____   E — $2\frac{7}{8}$" _____   I — $11\frac{9}{16}$" _____

B — $10\frac{3}{8}$" _____   F — $1\frac{1}{2}$" _____   J — $6\frac{3}{4}$" _____

C — $3\frac{1}{16}$" _____   G — $5\frac{13}{16}$" _____   K — $7\frac{7}{8}$" _____

D — $9\frac{11}{16}$" _____   H — $4\frac{1}{4}$" _____   L — $8\frac{5}{16}$" _____

A.   Read the following marks on the ruler.

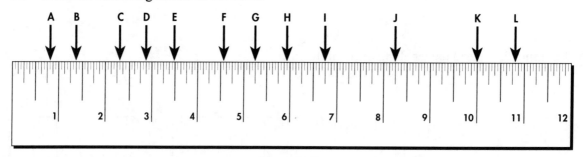

Figure 7-5

A = _____   E = _____   I = _____

B = _____   F = _____   J = _____

C = _____   G = _____   K = _____

D = _____   H = _____   L = _____

B. Draw a line beneath each measure of the appropriate length.

$2\frac{1}{8}$"

$1\frac{5}{16}$"

$4\frac{3}{4}$"

$7\frac{5}{8}$"

$6\frac{1}{2}$"

4"

$3\frac{15}{16}$"

Chapter 8

Metric System

Explaining the Metric System

The metric system is a system of measurement based on the number ten. There are ten smaller units in each larger unit. The metric system has three basic units of measure:

- the gram   (measures mass or weight)
- the liter   (measures volume or liquid)
- the meter   (measures length or distance)

Each of the units can be multiplied by ten to produce increasingly larger units or divided by ten to produce smaller units.

Let's look at the meter. It is $39\frac{3}{8}$" long. It is similar in size to a yardstick. It can be used to measure the length of a car or the height of an adult, but it is not useful for measuring the size of a sheet of paper or a paperclip. We need a smaller unit of measure. If we divide the meter by ten, it produces a unit called a decimeter. This can be used to measure smaller items. For very small items, we may measure in millimeters (which is a meter divided by 1,000, or a meter divided by 10 three times.) For very large items or distances, we may measure in kilometers (which is a meter multiplied by 1,000, or multiplied by 10 three times.) (See Figure 8-1)

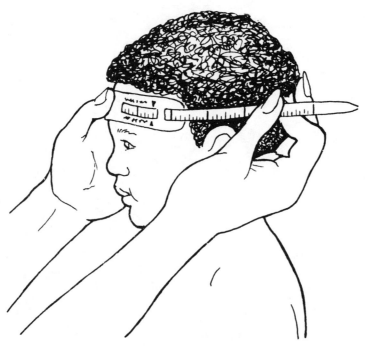

FIGURE 8-1 Measuring a head (From Keir, *MEDICAL ASSISTING,* 2nd ed., Copyright 1989 by Delmar Publishers Inc.)

The various length measurements are:

kilometer   hectometer   dekameter   meter   decimeter   centimeter   millimeter

LARGER <---> SMALLER

The various volume measurements are:

kiloliter   hectoliter   dekaliter   liter   deciliter   centiliter   milliliter

LARGER <--> SMALLER

The various mass measurements are:

kilogram   hectogram   dekagram   gram   decigram   centigram   milligram

LARGER <--> SMALLER

The three types of measurement are interrelated in the metric system. For example if you made a cube that measured one cent**imeter** and filled it with water, the amount it would hold is one milli**liter**. Then if you weighed that cube of water, it would weigh one **gram**, Figure 8-2.

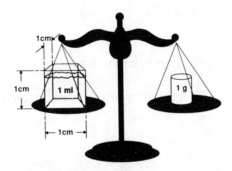

FIGURE 8-2 Scale (From Dunlap/*MATHEMATICS FOR HEALTH OCCUPATIONS,* Copyright 1991 by Delmar Publishers Inc.)

Prefixes and Abbreviations

The gram, meter, and liter are considered the base for each measurement. Any larger or smaller measurement is shown by using a prefix in front of these words (as shown on the previous page). Let's look more closely at the prefixes:

- kilo-   base × 1,000
- hecto-   base × 100
- deka-   base ×   10

BASE (meter, liter, or gram)

- deci-   base /   10
- centi-   base / 100
- milli-   base / 1,000

OR, another way of looking at this list is:

- kilo-   base × 1,000
- hecto-   base ×   100
- deka-   base ×   10

BASE (meter, liter, or gram)

- deci-   base × 0.1
- centi-   base × 0.01
- milli-   base × 0.001

To save time and standardize the use of metrics, abbreviations are often used. The abbreviations for the base units are:

meter = m   liter = l   gram = g

The abbreviations for the prefixes are:

kilo = k   deci = d
hecto = h   centi = c
deka = dk   milli = m

A prefix can never be used alone. It must have a base unit with it to indicate whether you are measuring length, volume, or mass.

Therefore, the abbreviations for the prefixes above must be combined with an abbreviation for a based unit as follows:

Length (See Figure 8–3)

kilometer = km
hectometer = hm
dekameter = dkm
meter = m
decimeter = dm
centimeter = cm
millimeter = mm

*Notice that m alone always means meter, since milli- cannot stand alone.

FIGURE 8–3 Metric length
(From Dunlap/*MATHEMATICS FOR HEALTH OCCUPATIONS*,
Copyright 1991 by Delmar Publishers Inc.)

Volume (See Figure 8-4)

kiloliter	=	kl
hectoliter	=	hl
dekaliter	=	dkl
liter	=	l
deciliter	=	dl
centiliter	=	cl
milliliter	=	ml

FIGURE 8-4 Metric volume
(From Dunlap/*MATHEMATICS FOR
HEALTH OCCUPATIONS,*
Copyright 1991 by Delmar Publishers Inc.)

Mass (See Figure 8-5)

kilogram	=	kg
hectogram	=	hg
dekagram	=	dkg
gram	=	g
decigram	=	dg
centigram	=	cg
milligram	=	mg

FIGURE 8-5 Metric mass
(From Dunlap/*MATHEMATICS FOR
HEALTH OCCUPATIONS,*
Copyright 1991 by Delmar Publishers Inc.)

Problems

1) Fill in the abbreviations for the following.

   a. kilogram   _____   f. centigram   _____

   b. deciliter   _____   g. hectoliter   _____

   c. dekameter   _____   h. milligram   _____

   d. liter   _____   i. gram   _____

   e. millimeter _____   j. dekaliter   _____

2) Match the base unit with what it measures by drawing a connecting line:

   meter   volume

   liter   mass

   gram   length

3) Using abbreviations, fill in the appropriate measurement for each of these descriptions.

a. 1,000 grams _____   f. 10 meters   _____

b. 100 liters   _____   g. 1/100 liter _____

c. 1/10 meter   _____   h. 1,000 meters _____

d. 1/1,000 liter _____   i. 10 grams   _____

e. 1 gram   _____   j. 1 liter   _____

Conversions in the Metric System

It is important in working with metric measurements to be able to convert from one measure to another. For example, how many centimeters are in a hectometer? Or, how many milliliters are in a liter?

Because all of the measurements are related by the number ten, we can convert measurements by moving the decimal.

Example 1:

1) Let's find out how many centimeters are in a hectometer. This can be rewritten as: 1 hm = _____ cm. This takes us from what we are given (1 hm) to what we are trying to find (how many cm's).

2) We need our list of measurements for length, Figure 8-6.

km   hm   dkm   m   dm   cm   mm

FIGURE 8-6 (From Dunlap/*MATHEMATICS FOR HEALTH OCCUPATIONS*,
Copyright 1991 by Delmar Publishers Inc.)

3) To convert from hm to cm we are going 4 units to the right. This means we should move our decimal 4 places to the right. Remember that in a whole number, the decimal begins at the right of the number, Figure 8-7.

1.0000 ——————— 10,000

FIGURE 8-7 (From Dunlap/*MATHEMATICS FOR HEALTH OCCUPATIONS*,
Copyright 1991 by Delmar Publishers Inc.)

4) So, 1 hm = _10,000_ cm

Example 2: How many milliliters are in 6.9 liters?

1) First restate the problem as 6.9 l = _____ml

2) Write down the list of measurements for volume.

kl   hl   dkl   l   dl   cl   ml

3) Determine the number of units you are moving and in which direction, Figure 8-8.

kl   hl   dkl   l   dl   cl   ml   * 3 to right

FIGURE 8-8 (From Dunlap/*MATHEMATICS FOR HEALTH OCCUPATIONS,*
Copyright 1991 by Delmar Publishers Inc.)

4) Move the decimal that number of places in the same direction, Figure 8-9.

6.900 ———————— 6,900

FIGURE 8-9 (From Dunlap/*MATHEMATICS FOR HEALTH OCCUPATIONS,*
Copyright 1991 by Delmar Publishers Inc.)

5) So, 6.9 l = _6,900_ ml

Example 3: How many hg are in 423 dg?

1) Restate the problem. (Notice that the words "how many" point us to what we are trying to find.)
   423 dg = _____ hg

2) Write down the list of measurements for mass.

   kg   hg   dkg   g   dg   cg   mg

3) Determine the number of units you are moving and in which direction, Figure 8-10.

kg   hg   dkg   g   dg   cg   mg

FIGURE 8-10 (From Dunlap/*MATHEMATICS FOR HEALTH OCCUPATIONS,*
Copyright 1991 by Delmar Publishers Inc.)

4) Move the decimal that number of places in the same direction, Figure 8-11.

423. ———————— .423

FIGURE 8-11 (From Dunlap/*MATHEMATICS FOR HEALTH OCCUPATIONS,*
Copyright 1991 by Delmar Publishers Inc.)

5) So, 423 dg = _.423_ hg

Volume Measurement

In converting volume measurements, you will always need the list of volume measurements.

kl   hl   dkl   l   dl   cl   ml

1) 29 dkl   = _____ dl
2) 18.6 l   = _____ ml
3) 37,423 ml   = _____ dl
4) 56.2 kl   = _____ hl
5) .14 l   = _____ cl
6) 83.92 cl   = _____ hl
7) 6 dkl   = _____ l
8) 15 dl   = _____ ml

9) 2,947 ml   = _____ cl
10) 24.7 dkl   = _____ kl
11) 932.6 l   = _____ hl
12) 46.5 dl   = _____ cl
13) .26 cl   = _____ dkl
14) 4.553 l   = _____ dl
15) 811.6 kl   = _____ hl

In #16–#20 be sure to restate the problem as shown in the examples.

16) How many dl are in 16 l?   _____
17) An hl equals how many l?   _____
18) How many dekaliters are in 276.8 deciliters?   _____
19) How many milliliters are in a 2 liter bottle?   _____
20) How many hl are in 27 dkl?   _____

Length Measurement

In converting length measurements, you will always need the list of length measurements.

km   hm   dkm   m   dm   cm   mm

1) 187.6 km   = _____ dkm
2) 2965 cm   = _____ m
3) 42.5 hm   = _____ km
4) 19,653 cm   = _____ dkm
5) 29 m   = _____ mm
6) 14.37 hm   = _____ dm
7) 49.8 cm   = _____ hm
8) 2963 mm   = _____ dm

9) 43 km   = _____ m
10) 8.167 m   = _____ cm
11) 14,382 hm = _____ km
12) 9 mm   = _____ dm
13) 7,676 dm   = _____ hm
14) 2.96 km   = _____ dkm
15) 1.119 cm   = _____ mm

In #16–#20 be sure to restate the problem as shown in the examples.

16) How many m are in a km?   _____
17) How many dekameters are in 6,921 centimeters?   _____
18) 18 dkm equals how many mm?   _____
19) A person 17.5 dm tall is how many meters tall?   _____
20) How many decimeters are in 2.8 hectometers?   _____

Mass Measurement

In converting mass measurements you will always need the list of mass measurements.

	kg	hg	dkg	g	dg	cg	mg

1) 8.63 kg = _____ g

2) 49,682 cg = _____ dkg

3) 425 dg = _____ dkg

4) 84.1 hg = _____ cg

5) 436 kg = _____ mg

6) 89,632 mg = _____ cg

7) 42.31 dkg = _____ kg

8) 5.85 mg = _____ dg

9) 863 g = _____ cg

10) 2,111 hg = _____ dg

11) 91.164 cg = _____ hg

12) 4 g = _____ kg

13) 56.11 dg = _____ dkg

14) 81 kg = _____ hg

15) 534 g = _____ mg

In #16–#20 be sure to restate the problems as shown in the examples.

16) How many cg are in 15 dkg? _____

17) How many grams are in 4.65 kilograms? _____

18) How many mg are in a gram? _____

19) How many dg are in 4 hg? _____

20) How many kilograms are in 1654 dekagrams? _____

Metric/English Conversions

Often in our use of the metric system it is helpful to know the relationship of metric measurements to their English counterparts.

To convert from one system to the other it is necessary to know some conversion facts (these are the approximations most commonly used):

Volume

1 quart = 1 liter = 1,000 ml or cc
1 pint = 500 ml or cc
1 cup = 240 ml or cc
1 ounce = 30 ml or cc
1 tbl. = 15 ml or cc
1 tsp. = 5 ml or cc

Length

1 mile = 1601.6 m
1 yard = .91 m
1 foot = .31 m
1 inch = .025 m

Mass

1 pound = .454 kg
1 ounce = .028 kg

One simple rule is also helpful. When changing English units to metric using the above conversion facts, multiply by the appropriate conversion number. When changing metric to English, divide.

$$\text{English} \rightarrow \text{metric} = \text{multiply}$$
$$\text{metric} \rightarrow \text{English} = \text{divide}$$

Example 1: How many ml are in 4 pints?

1) Restate the problem.

    4 pt. = _____ ml

2) This is English to metric, so multiply.

3) Determine which conversions fact to use (1 pt = 500 ml).

4) 4 pt. × 500 ml = 2000 ml

5) So, 4 pt. = _2000_ ml

Example 2: How many meters are in 100 yards?

1) Restate the problem.

    100 yds. = _____m

2) English to metric, so multiply.

3) Determine which conversion fact to use (1 yd. = .91 m).

4) 100 yd. × .91 m = 91

5) So, 100 yds. = _91_ m

Example 3: How many pounds are in 68.1 kg?

1) Restate the problem.

    68.1 kg = _____ lb

2) Metric to English, so divide.

3) Determine which conversion fact to use (1 lb = .454 kg).

4) 68.1 kg / .454 kg = 150

5) So, 68.1 kg = _150_ lb

Problems   Complete the following conversions.

1) a. 4 tsp.   = _____ ml   e. 2.25 pts. = _____ ml

    b. 3 oz.   = _____ ml   f. 3 tsp.   = _____ ml

    c. 1.5 c   = _____ ml   g. 4 c.   = _____ ml

    d. 13 tbl. = _____ ml   h. 10 tbl.   = _____ ml

2) a. 270 ml = _____ oz.   e. 1 ml   = _____tsp.

   b. 45 ml   = _____ tsp.   f. 90 ml = _____ tbl.

   c. 3000 ml = _____ pt.   g. 45 ml = _____ oz.

   d. 1920 ml = _____ c   h. 120 ml = _____ c

3) a. 6 yds. = _____ m

   b. 20 in. = _____ m

   c. 2 ft.   = _____ m

   d. 6 in.   = _____ m

4) a. 3.1 m   = _____ ft.

   b. 75 m   = _____ in.

   c. 1.365 m = _____ yd.

   d. 1.55 m = _____ ft.

5) a. 6 lb.   = _____ kg

   b. 150 lb. = _____ kg

   c. 16 oz. = _____ kg

   d. 4 oz.   = _____ kg

6) a. 2.66 kg = _____ oz.

   b. 2.8 kg = _____ oz.

   c. 27.24 kg = _____ lb.

   d. 4.086 kg = _____ lb.

Chapter 9

Geometry

Angles

A cosmetologist uses angles to determine how to roll hair. The amount of lift you want or the direction you want the curl to take will determine at what angle you will roll the hair.

This chapter will give you practice in recognizing angles and being able to identify common angles.

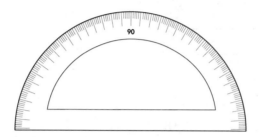

FIGURE 9-1 Protractor

This is a protractor, Figure 9-1. It is used in mathematics to show the degrees of a circle. Every circle has 360°. Every half circle then has 180°. The protractor is read right to left, with zero degrees being on the bottom right and 180 degrees being on the bottom left. The marks around the outside of the half-circle indicate degrees and every fifth degree is marked by a slightly longer line. This helps you to be able to read it more accurately.

A protractor can be used to read angles that already exist or to help you in drawing angles. To read an angle place the bottom of the half-circle on the bottom line of the angle and determine to what degree the other line of the angle extends. To draw an angle, draw a straight line and set the protractor on that line. Draw a small mark above the degree of angle you wish to draw and another at the midpoint of the protractor's bottom edge. Remove the protractor and use the straight edge of the protractor to connect the two small marks you have made.

Example 1: Read the following angle.

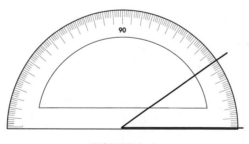

FIGURE 9-2

Since the second line of the angle extends through 35°, this is a 35 degree angle.

76

Example 2:   Draw a 75° angle.

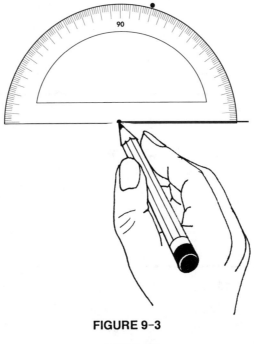

FIGURE 9-3

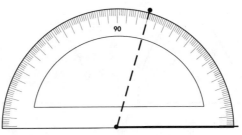

FIGURE 9-4

Problems   Read the following angles.

1)

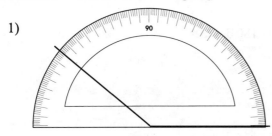

FIGURE 9-5

3)

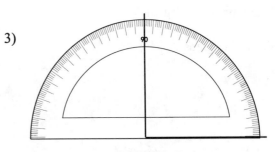

FIGURE 9-7

2)

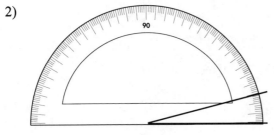

FIGURE 9-6

4)

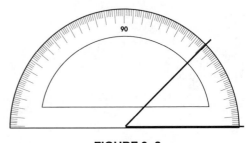

FIGURE 9-8

5)

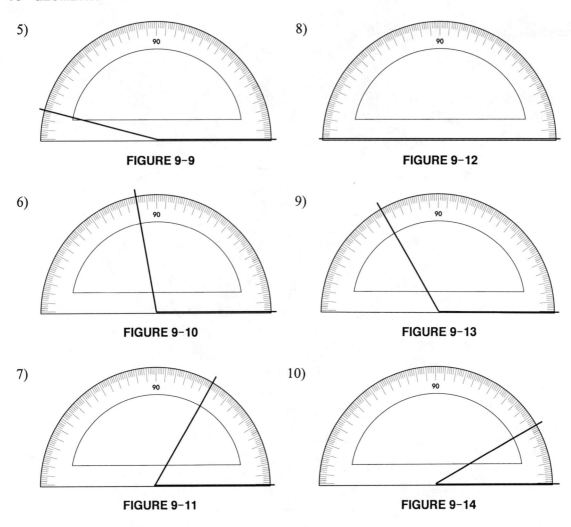

FIGURE 9-9

8)

FIGURE 9-12

6)

FIGURE 9-10

9)

FIGURE 9-13

7)

FIGURE 9-11

10)

FIGURE 9-14

Draw the following angles.

11) 115 degrees

14) 180 degrees

12) 45 degrees

15) 135 degrees

13) 90 degrees

16) 70 degrees

17) 20 degrees   19) 30 degrees

18) 105 degrees   20) 150 degrees

Chapter 10

Money

Handling Money

Handling money is an essential skill for every kind of cosmetology occupation. Most cosmetologists will at some time need to make change, collect payments, make bank deposits, or sort money.

Money is exchanged in many different forms. It can be currency (bills and coins), checks, money orders, or traveler's checks. Each kind is handled a little differently and should be kept separate in a cash drawer, Figure 10-1.

FIGURE 10-1

First, when handling currency it is helpful to turn all of the bills face up and in one direction as you receive them. Also, keep the largest denominations as far away from the customer's access as possible when placing the money in your cash drawer.

When handling coins be careful to sort them accurately when placing them in the cash drawer, again keeping the largest denominations as far away from the customer's access as possible.

When handling checks it is important to go over the check when you receive it to be sure it has been written correctly. Most agencies examine the check for correct address and phone number, correct date, accurate amount (in number and in words), and a complete signature, Figure 10-2.

Other information may be requested and recorded on the back of the check such as driver's license number, social security number, or credit card numbers.

In addition, some agencies endorse the check immediately (For Deposit Only—Dayton Salon) so that it cannot be cashed if it is stolen. Money orders are treated much the same as checks.

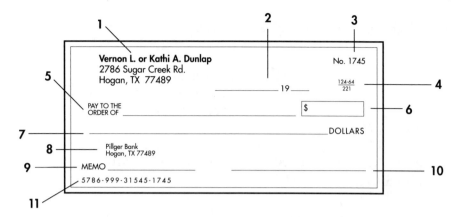

1 Name and address of person(s) holding bank account
2 Date check is written
3 Number of the check
4 Bank identification number
5 Payee of check (person to whom check is written)
6 Amount of check in numbers
7 Amount of check, expressed in words
8 Bank where checking account is held
9 Memo line (reason for writing check)
10 Signature of person writing check
11 Checking account number (last 4 digits indicate check number (item 3) again)

FIGURE 10-2

Traveler's checks would rarely be seen in a beauty shop (since most of your customers would have no reason to use traveler's checks in their own town.) They can be received, however, and should be signed by the customer in your presence when you receive them. This signature should match the corresponding signature already on the traveler's check.

Making Change

Whenever a customer pays for the services rendered, he may or may not give you the exact payment. If the exact payment is given, accept the money, write the receipt (introduced later in this chapter), and thank the customer. If exact payment is not given, accept the money, make correct change, write the receipt, and thank the customer.

Making the correct change is essential. Giving too much change will result in a lack of money in your cash drawer at the end of the day. Giving too little change will create ill-will with your customers.

To give change, begin with what they owed you and add to that until you reach the amount they paid. For example, the bill comes to $27 and they give you two $20s ($40 total). Begin at $27 mentally, give them three $1s ($27 + $3 = $30). Now that you are at $30 mentally, give them a $10 ($30 + $10 = $40). You have reached $40, so your change is complete. To check, the bill ($27) plus the change ($13) should equal the payment ($40).

BILL + CHANGE GIVEN = PAYMENT

Example 1:   The bill is $6.50. They give you a $20.

SAY...

		6.50	(begin mentally)
give	.25	6.75	(trying to get to an even dollar amount)
give	.25	7.00	(now use $1 bills)
give	1.00	8.00	
give	1.00	9.00	(trying to get to an even $10)
give	1.00	10.00	(now use two $5s or a $10 bill)
give	10.00	20.00	
	13.50		

Check: 6.50 (bill) + 13.50 (change) = $20 (payment)

Example 2:   The bill is $4.79. They give you a $10.

SAY...

		4.79	(begin mentally)
give	.01	4.80	(now you can use dimes)
give	.10	4.90	(trying to get to an even dollar amt.)
give	.10	5.00	(now use a $5 bill or five $1s)
give	5.00	10.00	
	5.21		

Check: 4.79 (bill) + 5.21 (change) = $10 (payment)

Problems   Use only the spaces needed to complete each problem.

1) The bill is $29. They give you two $20s.

SAY...

give _____   _____

give _____   _____

give _____   _____

give _____   _____

2) The bill is $3.50. They give you a $20.

SAY...

give _____   _____

give _____   _____

give _____   _____

give _____   _____

give _____   _____

give _____   _____

3) The bill is $6.95. They give you a $10.

SAY...

            _____

give _____   _____

give _____   _____

give _____   _____

give _____   _____

give _____   _____

give _____   _____

4) The bill is $18. They give you a $50.

SAY...

            _____ 18

give __8)__   __19__

give __$3__   __2?__

give __$10\_\_   \_\_$ 42__

give __$3__   __45__

give __$5__   __50__

5) The bill is $2.88. They give you a $10.

SAY...

            _____

give _____   _____

give _____   _____

give _____   _____

give _____   _____

give _____   _____

give _____   _____

6) The bill is $26.69. They give you a $20 and a $10.

SAY...

            _____

give _____   _____

give _____   _____

give _____   _____

give _____   _____

give _____   _____

give _____   _____

7) The bill is $86.75. They give you five $20s.

SAY...

_____

give _____   _____

give _____   _____

give _____   _____

give _____   _____

give _____   _____

give _____   _____

8) The bill is $14.60. They give you a $10 and a $5.

SAY...

_____

give _____   _____

give _____   _____

give _____   _____

give _____   _____

give _____   _____

give _____   _____

9) The bill is $39.00. They give you two $20s.

SAY...

_____

give _____   _____

give _____   _____

give _____   _____

give _____   _____

give _____   _____

10)   The bill is $106.15. They give you six $20s.

SAY...

give _____   _____

give _____   _____

give _____   _____

give _____   _____

give _____   _____

give _____   _____

give _____   _____

give _____   _____

In problems #11−#20, write in order what coins or bills you would give.

Example: Bill   = $14.55   3455
                  Given   = $20.00   5000
                                            8 035
                                   34.55

$.10 $.10 $.25 $5.00 _____   _____   _____   _____   _____   _____   _____

11)   Bill   = $21.05
      Given   = $25.00

_____   _____   _____   _____   _____   _____   _____   _____   _____   _____

12)   Bill   = $23.45
      Given   = $25.00

_____   _____   _____   _____   _____   _____   _____   _____   _____   _____

13)   Bill   = $47.09
      Given   = $50.00

_____   _____   _____   _____   _____   _____   _____   _____   _____   _____

14)   Bill   = $116.48
      Given   = $120.00

_____   _____   _____   _____   _____   _____   _____   _____   _____   _____

15)   Bill   = $18.80
      Given   = $50.00

_____   _____   _____   _____   _____   _____   _____   _____   _____   _____

16)   Bill   = $43.75
      Given   = $60.00

_____   _____   _____   _____   _____   _____   _____   _____   _____   _____

17) Bill   = $ 9.00
    Given = $20.00

_____

18) Bill   = $ 57.40
    Given = $100.00

_____

19) Bill   = $23.95
    Given = $30.00

_____

20) Bill   = $74.20
    Given = $75.00

_____

Writing Receipts

In the cosmetology profession, receipts often serve two purposes. The first is to record what services the client would like to have completed when they first arrive (perm, shampoo and set, etc.). The main purpose, then, is to provide a written record of the total cost of services. A copy of this can be kept for clients and the original is kept with the salon. It normally contains spaces for the following information:

- date
- services desired
- name of customer
- address

- method of payment
- operator

Name	Barbara Eversole		
Address	1520 Hudson Pkwy.		
	Tyler, PA 41106		
Cash Ck Chg	Operator KD	Next Appt.	
2–15–92	Shampoo & Set		7.00
		Subtotal	7.00
		Tax	
		Total	7.00

FIGURE 10–3

When writing receipts, you must be able to figure out what the customer owes. This is called the **current balance**. To find their current balance use the following formula:

CURRENT BALANCE = SERVICES RENDERED + OTHER PRODUCTS PURCHASED

Problems   Complete the following information on the receipts. Be sure to sign your name on the receipts where this is called for.

1) Jack Elliott came into your shop for a cut and style. The charge for this is $15. He paid cash. Today's date is 8/17/--. His address is 1510 Clermont Street, Grange, IL.

Name			
Address			
Cash Ck Chg	Operator _____	Next Appt.	
		Subtotal	
		Tax	
		Total	

FIGURE 10-4

2) Nola Leven sent a check for payment of $45.25 to your shop today for a tanning membership she wishes to buy. Today's date is 7/11/--. She would like you to send her a receipt. Her address is 512 Clowton St, Grange, IL.

Name			
Address			
Cash Ck Chg	Operator _____	Next Appt.	
		Subtotal	
		Tax	
		Total	

FIGURE 10-4

3) Karen Hines came in today for a permanent. The charge for that is $36.50. She paid by check.
Today's date is 4/15/--. Her address is 2191 East Pemberton, Freemont, IL.

Name				
Address				
Cash Ck Chg	Operator _____		Next Appt.	
			Subtotal	
			Tax	
			Total	

FIGURE 10-4

4) Greg Bercoff came in for a cut and style ($15.00). He also bought hair conditioner ($7.45).
Today's date is 4/17/--. His address is 1200 Trail Ridge Road, Grange, IL. He is a long-time
customer and has an in-house account.

Name				
Address				
Cash Ck Chg	Operator _____		Next Appt.	
			Subtotal	
			Tax	
			Total	

FIGURE 10-4

5) Sarah Mullenston came in today for a manicure and color tint. The charge for the manicure is $6.50 and the charge for the tint is $32.75. She wrote a check. Write her a receipt. Today's date is 5/18/--. Her address is 621 Covington Place, Freemont, IL.

Name			
Address			
Cash Ck Chg	Operator _____	Next Appt.	
		Subtotal	
		Tax	
		Total	

FIGURE 10-4

6) Hugh Golliver came in today and bought some hair care items for his wife as a gift. He bought Determine shampoo ($6.95), Style Plus III styling gel ($5.29), and Coifure Hair Spray ($7.90) for cash. Today is 2/14/--. His address is 551 Wayne Blvd, Grange, IL. Charge 5% tax on all products.

Name			
Address			
Cash Ck Chg	Operator _____	Next Appt.	
		Subtotal	
		Tax	
		Total	

FIGURE 10-4

7) Randy Cramer came in today and paid cash for a tanning session costing $4.75. Today is 3/29/-- and his address is 4487 Golliver Street, Grange IL

Name				
Address				
Cash Ck Chg	Operator _____	Next Appt.		
		Subtotal		
		Tax		
		Total		

FIGURE 10-4

8) Donna Myers (a long time customer with an account) came in today for a permanent. She owes $42.00 for today's services. She also decided to purchase a new brush for $4.95 and some shampoo for $6.95. She lives at 41 Cheshire Circle, Freemont, IL. Today is 5/5/--. Charge 5% tax on all products.

Name				
Address				
Cash Ck Chg	Operator _____	Next Appt.		
		Subtotal		
		Tax		
		Total		

FIGURE 10-4

9) Sean Sanders came in today for a haircut and paid cash. Because of special techniques used, he is charged for a basic cut ($7.50) and an additional $1.75. Today is 9/9/--. He lives at 9293 Farmington Road, Grange, IL.

Name			
Address			
Cash Ck Chg	Operator _____	Next Appt.	
		Subtotal	
		Tax	
		Total	

FIGURE 10-4

10) Marie Hill came in today for a facial, which she paid for by check. Her charge for the facial is $5.95. Today is 6/17/--. She lives at 263 Holman Avenue, Freemont, IL.

Name			
Address			
Cash Ck Chg	Operator _____	Next Appt.	
		Subtotal	
		Tax	
		Total	

FIGURE 10-4

Balancing a Cash Drawer

When all money has been received for the day, a bank deposit must be prepared. Before the money can be deposited, however, a cashier count sheet must be completed to determine if the amount collected from customers is correct, Figure 10-5.

Daily Balance Sheet

Date: _____

NUMBER	DENOMINATION	AMOUNT
	Pennies	
	Nickels	
	Dimes	
	Quarters	
	Half Dollars	
	$1 Bills	
	$5 Bills	
	$10 Bills	
	$20 Bills	
	Checks	
	Cash in Drawer	
	Plus Cash Paid Out	
	Total Cash	
	Less Change	
	Cash Received, Cashier's Count	
	Cash Received, Ledger Count	
	AMOUNT OF CASH SHORT OR OVER	

Cash Proved _____   Cash Over _____   Cash Short _____

FIGURE 10-5

To complete the cashier count sheet, first separate checks, money orders, traveler's checks, and cash. You should then count how many of each different coin and bill you have. This information is recorded in the left hand column under **number**. When this has been done (and double checked), set the money aside. Next, multiply the number of coins or bills by the value of that coin or bill. This gives you the **amount** to be recorded in the right hand column. The checks, money orders, and traveler's checks should be counted next and then the value of these items should be totalled. Set checks, money orders, and traveler's checks aside.

After this count, all amounts should be totalled together to determine **cash in drawer**.

Any **cash paid outs** (money paid from the cash drawer for deliveries, etc.) should be written on the next line and added to the cash in drawer to determine **total cash**.

Next, write the amount of cash you began the day with (petty cash for making change) in **less change** and subtract it from the total cash to determine **cash received, cashier's count**.

This is the amount that you, as cashier, have collected that day. After this is complete, write in the amount of collection that your cash register or customer receipts indicates was collected that day on the **cash received, ledger** line. Then compare your cashier count with the ledger amount. If the cashier count is the smaller amount, you are short of funds. If the cashier count is larger, you are over. If the amount is the same, it is said that your cash "proved." Identify whether you are short, over, or proved and check the appropriate line. Then subtract the two amounts to find the difference. Write this amount at the bottom of the form in **Amount of Cash Short or Over**.

Problems   Complete these cashier count sheets using the following information:

1) PENNIES 37
    NICKELS 16
    DIMES   30
    QUARTERS 19
    HALF DOLLARS 0
    $ 1 BILLS 41
    $ 5 BILLS 7
    $10 BILLS 5
    $20 BILLS 6
    $50 BILLS 0
    CHECKS .... 5 totalling $147.89

    CASH PAID OUT .... $ 4.25
    BEGINNING CHANGE 40.00
    CASH RECEIVED ACCORDING
        TO CUSTOMER RECEIPTS OR
        CASH REGISTER 376.06

Daily Balance Sheet

Date: _____

NUMBER	DENOMINATION	AMOUNT
	Pennies	
	Nickels	
	Dimes	
	Quarters	
	Half Dollars	
	$1 Bills	
	$5 Bills	
	$10 Bills	
	$20 Bills	
	Checks	
	Cash in Drawer	
	Plus Cash Paid Out	
	Total Cash	
	Less Change	
	Cash Received, Cashier's Count	
	Cash Received, Ledger Count	
	AMOUNT OF CASH SHORT OR OVER	

Cash Proved _____   Cash Over _____   Cash Short _____

FIGURE 10-5

2)

PENNIES	26
NICKELS	15
DIMES	17
QUARTERS	21
HALF DOLLARS	0
$ 1 BILLS	18
$ 5 BILLS	9
$10 BILLS	8
$20 BILLS	5
$50 BILLS	0
CHECKS	5 totalling $189.10

CASH PAID OUT .... $ 7.15
BEGINNING CHANGE 25.00
CASH RECEIVED ACCORDING
    TO CUSTOMER RECEIPTS OR
    CASH REGISTER 422.21

Daily Balance Sheet

Date: _____

NUMBER	DENOMINATION	AMOUNT
	Pennies	
	Nickels	
	Dimes	
	Quarters	
	Half Dollars	
	$1 Bills	
	$5 Bills	
	$10 Bills	
	$20 Bills	
	Checks	
	Cash in Drawer	
	Plus Cash Paid Out	
	Total Cash	
	Less Change	
	Cash Received, Cashier's Count	
	Cash Received, Ledger Count	
	AMOUNT OF CASH SHORT OR OVER	

Cash Proved _____   Cash Over _____   Cash Short _____

FIGURE 10-5

3) PENNIES 20
    NICKELS 17
    DIMES   12
    QUARTERS 19
    HALF DOLLARS 0
    $ 1 BILLS 27
    $ 5 BILLS 16
    $10 BILLS 14
    $20 BILLS 7
    $50 BILLS 0
    CHECKS   .... 6 totalling $210.00

CASH PAID OUT .... $ 1.30
BEGINNING CHANGE 40.00
CASH RECEIVED ACCORDING
    TO CUSTOMER RECEIPTS OR
    CASH REGISTER 570.30

Daily Balance Sheet

Date: _____

NUMBER	DENOMINATION	AMOUNT
	Pennies	
	Nickels	
	Dimes	
	Quarters	
	Half Dollars	
	$1 Bills	
	$5 Bills	
	$10 Bills	
	$20 Bills	
	Checks	
	Cash in Drawer	
	Plus Cash Paid Out	
	Total Cash	
	Less Change	
	Cash Received, Cashier's Count	
	Cash Received, Ledger Count	
	AMOUNT OF CASH SHORT OR OVER	

Cash Proved _____   Cash Over _____   Cash Short _____

FIGURE 10–5

4)
PENNIES	....	13
NICKELS	....	19
DIMES	....	21
QUARTERS	....	40
HALF DOLLARS	....	0
$ 1 BILLS	....	17
$ 5 BILLS	....	8
$10 BILLS	....	6
$20 BILLS	....	5
$50 BILLS	....	0
CHECKS	....	5 totalling $174.00

CASH PAID OUT .... $ 7.70
BEGINNING CHANGE........................ 20.00
CASH RECEIVED ACCORDING
   TO CUSTOMER RECEIPTS OR
   CASH REGISTER 390.88

Daily Balance Sheet

Date: _____

NUMBER	DENOMINATION	AMOUNT
	Pennies	
	Nickels	
	Dimes	
	Quarters	
	Half Dollars	
	$1 Bills	
	$5 Bills	
	$10 Bills	
	$20 Bills	
	Checks	
	Cash in Drawer	
	Plus Cash Paid Out	
	Total Cash	
	Less Change	
	Cash Received, Cashier's Count	
	Cash Received, Ledger Count	
	AMOUNT OF CASH SHORT OR OVER	

Cash Proved _____   Cash Over _____   Cash Short _____

FIGURE 10–5

5) PENNIES   9
    NICKELS 12
    DIMES   11
    QUARTERS 17
    HALF DOLLARS.   0
    $ 1 BILLS 25
    $ 5 BILLS 10
    $10 BILLS 11
    $20 BILLS   7
    $50 BILLS   0
    CHECKS ....   4 totalling $110.50

CASH PAID OUT .... $ 6.00
BEGINNING CHANGE 35.00
CASH RECEIVED ACCORDING
    TO CUSTOMER RECEIPTS OR
    CASH REGISTER 302.04

	Daily Balance Sheet		
Date: _____		
NUMBER	DENOMINATION	AMOUNT
	Pennies	
	Nickels	
	Dimes	
	Quarters	
	Half Dollars	
	$1 Bills	
	$5 Bills	
	$10 Bills	
	$20 Bills	
	Checks	
	Cash in Drawer	
	Plus Cash Paid Out	
	Total Cash	
	Less Change	
	Cash Received, Cashier's Count	
	Cash Received, Ledger Count	
	AMOUNT OF CASH SHORT OR OVER	

Cash Proved _____   Cash Over _____   Cash Short _____

FIGURE 10–5

Chapter 11

Time

Elapsed Time

Elapsed time is the amount of time that has passed from one moment to another. We often use elapsed time without thinking much about it. For example, in a beauty shop it may be used to determine when to schedule the next appointment or how long to leave a permanent in place. These are common uses of elapsed time that can often be figured mentally. Another use of elapsed time in some cosmetology careers is determining how long an employee has been at work. This information is needed to compute the employee's paycheck when the employee is paid on an hourly basis.

To figure elapsed time there are a few basic rules:

1. Put the ending (or leaving) time on top of the starting (or arrival) time as for a subtraction problem. Separate the hours from the minutes with a vertical line.
2. Subtract the minutes. If you are unable to and need to borrow, borrow one hour from the hours and add that hour (as 60 minutes now) to the minutes. Then subtract.
3. Next, subtract the hours. If you are unable to subtract then add 12 hours (a full rotation around the clock). Then subtract.

Example 1: Find the elapsed time from 9:11 am to 3:15 pm.

1) $\begin{array}{r} 3: \\ -9: \end{array} \begin{array}{|l} 15 \\ 11 \end{array}$ Set up subtraction and draw a vertical line. (NOTE: This is *not* 315 minus 911)

2) $\begin{array}{r} 3: \\ -9: \\ \hline \end{array} \begin{array}{|l} 15 \\ 11 \\ \hline 04 \end{array}$ Subtract minutes. $(15 - 11 = 4)$
Write as a 2-digit answer. (04)

3) $\begin{array}{r} \overset{15}{\cancel{3}}: \\ -9: \\ \hline 6: \end{array} \begin{array}{|l} 15 \\ 11 \\ \hline 04 \end{array}$ Subtract hours. $(3 - 9 = \text{impossible})$
If unable to, add 12 hours to 3, then subtract.

4) Elapsed time is 6 hours and 4 minutes. This may be written as 6:04 but remember that it does not mean 6:04 am or pm, it means a time of 6 hours and 4 minutes elapsed.

Example 2: Find the elapsed time from 1:14 pm to 9:29 pm.

1) $\begin{array}{r} 9: \\ -1: \end{array} \begin{array}{|l} 29 \\ 14 \end{array}$ Set up subtraction and draw a vertical line.

2) $\begin{array}{r} 9: \\ -1: \\ \hline \end{array} \begin{array}{|l} 29 \\ 14 \\ \hline 15 \end{array}$ Subtract minutes. $(29 - 14 = 15)$
Write as a 2-digit answer. (15)

3) $\begin{array}{r} 9: \\ -1: \\ \hline 8: \end{array} \begin{array}{|l} 29 \\ 14 \\ \hline 15 \end{array}$ Subtract hours. $(9 - 1 = 8)$

4) Elapsed time is 8 hours and 15 minutes.

Example 3: Find the elapsed time from 11:58 am to 5:05 pm.

1) $\begin{array}{r} 5: \,|\,05 \\ -\,11: \,|\,58 \end{array}$ Set up subtraction and draw a vertical line.

2) $\begin{array}{r} \mathbf{4}\ \ \mathbf{65} \\ \cancel{5}:\,|\,\cancel{05} \\ -\,11:\,|\,58 \\ \hline |\,07 \end{array}$ Subtract minutes. (5 − 58 = impossible) If unable to, borrow an hour (so 5 hours becomes 4) and add that hour (as 60 minutes) to the 5 minutes (60 + 5 = 65), then subtract.

3) $\begin{array}{r} \mathbf{16} \\ \cancel{4}\ \ \mathbf{65} \\ \cancel{5}:\,|\,\cancel{05} \\ -\,11:\,|\,58 \\ \hline 5:\,|\,07 \end{array}$ Subtract hours. (4 − 11 = impossible) If unable to, add 12 hours to 4, then subtract.

4) Elapsed time is 5 hours and 7 minutes.

Often when recording time for time sheets, employees will record only the time they are actually at work, excluding their lunch hour. To solve a problem like this compute elapsed time for the morning hours and then the evening hours and add them together. Be aware when adding minutes that any total which is larger than 59 minutes is not written as 60 minutes or more but as 1 hour or 1 hour and so many minutes instead.

Example 1: Find the total elapsed time from 8:07 am to 11:45 pm and 12:30 pm to 5:06 pm.

1) Morning hours

$\begin{array}{r} 11:\,|\,45 \\ -\ 8:\,|\,07 \\ \hline 3:\,|\,38 \end{array}$

Afternoon hours

$\begin{array}{r} \mathbf{16} \\ \cancel{4}\ \ \mathbf{66} \\ \cancel{5}:\,|\,\cancel{06} \\ -\,12:\,|\,30 \\ \hline 4:\,|\,36 \end{array}$

2) Add $\begin{array}{r} 3:\,|\,38 \\ +\ 4:\,|\,36 \\ \hline 7:\,|\,74 \\ \\ 8:\,|\,14 \end{array}$
- 74 minutes is 1 hour 14 minutes
- Add the 1 hour to the 7, and deduct 60 minutes from the 74

3) Solution is 8:14, 8 hours and 14 minutes.

Example 2: Find the total elapsed time from 7:09 am to 12:56 pm and 2:01 pm to 5:38 pm.

1) Morning hours
$\begin{array}{r} 12:\,|\,56 \\ -\ 7:\,|\,09 \\ \hline 5:\,|\,47 \end{array}$

Afternoon hours
$\begin{array}{r} 5:\,|\,58 \\ -\ 2:\,|\,01 \\ \hline 3:\,|\,57 \end{array}$

2) Add $\begin{array}{r} 5:\,|\,47 \\ +\ 3:\,|\,57 \\ \hline 8:\,|\,104 \\ \\ 9:\,|\,44 \end{array}$
- 104 minutes is 1 hour 44 minutes
- Add the 1 hour to the 8, and deduct 60 minutes from the 104

3) Solution is 9:44, 9 hours and 44 minutes.

Problems   Find the elapsed time.

1)	9:18 am to 3:15 pm	_____	6)	9:02 am to 5:11 pm	_____
2)	10:00 am to 5:48 pm	_____	7)	6:49 am to 12:08 pm	_____
3)	8:19 am to 3:30 pm	_____	8)	12:43 pm to 5:06 pm	_____
4)	9:00 am to 3:57 pm	_____	9)	11:40 am to 6:07 pm	_____
5)	7:58 am to 4:14 pm	_____	10)	7:45 am to 3:44 pm	_____

In problems #11–#15 find elapsed time for am and pm and add together.

	IN	OUT	IN	OUT		
11)	7:58	11:49	1:00	4:56	AM	_____
					PM	_____
					Total	_____
12)	8:01	12:51	1:30	4:19	AM	_____
					PM	_____
					Total	_____
13)	6:58	11:02	12:00	4:00	AM	_____
					PM	_____
					Total	_____
14)	7:00	11:30	12:15	4:30	AM	_____
					PM	_____
					Total	_____
15)	8:06	11:53	12:31	4:08	AM	_____
					PM	_____
					Total	_____

Time Sheets

In most states cosmetology students are required to keep a detailed written record of the time they spend learning various aspects of cosmetology. This written record is called a **time sheet.**

Although formats vary from state to state the same basic information is required. It is necessary to record the time that is spent in classroom instruction, in practice, and in actual client involvement. The time sheet we will use in this text records these hours as *theory, demonstration, practice,* and *clinic*—theory being the classroom instruction, demonstration being the hands-on examples of your instructor, practice being the assignments completed on a manniquin, and clinic being services rendered to clients. All time will be recorded in $\frac{1}{4}$ hour ($\frac{1}{4}$, $\frac{1}{2}$, $\frac{3}{4}$ or whole hour) segments.

It will be necessary to keep a weekly total of activities in the appropriate categories, but also to keep a running (accumulative) total. This accumulative total will help you as a student to determine when you have reached the number of hours required by your state board of cosmetology or similar agency.

Example 1: Carrie keeps track of the activities that she completes each day as a cosmetology student. Total the following activities and record on the time sheet, Figure 11-1.

Date	Lecture & Theory	Hr	Demonstration	Hr	Practice	Hr	Clinic	Hr
6/11	Haircutting	1 ¼	Haircutting	1 ¼	Haircutting	2		
6/12	Haircutting	1 ½	Haircutting	1	Haircutting	2		
6/13	Haircutting	1 ¼	Haircutting	2	Haircutting	1 ¼		
		4		4 ¼		5 ¼		

FIGURE 11-1

Example 2:   After keeping track of this week's activities, Carrie must transfer the appropriate number of hours into each section on the back of her time sheet. Then she must add this week's hours to her previous total to determine her accumulated total, Figure 11–2.

	THIS WEEK'S HOURS				THEORY		DEMO		PRACTICE		CLINIC	
	THEORY	DEMO	PRACTICE	CLINIC	BALANCE FORWARD	TOTAL	BALANCE FORWARD	TOTAL	BALANCE FORWARD	TOTAL	BALANCE FORWARD	TOTAL
I. CARE OF SCALP												
Scalp care					34	34	16½	16½	27	27		
Shampoo					16	16	13½	13½	20½	20½		
Rinses					11½	11½	7	7	16	16		
II. CARE OF HANDS												
Manicure— Water												
Oil.................................												
Electric												
Hand and arm bleach												
Hand and arm massage												
III. CARE OF HAIR												
Hair I.												
Hairstyling and Wigs	1¼	2	1¼		8½	9¾	8	10	11¼	12½		
Cutting, Trimming, etc.	2¾	2¼	4		7	9¾	6	8¼	7¾	11¾		
Hair II.												
Permanent waves, etc.												
Or, hair pressing and marcel												
Dyes, tints, bleaches, etc.												
IV. CARE OF FACE												
Facial and make-up												
Special masks and packs												
Eyebrow arching												
V. DISPENSARY												
DESK: Shop Management												
Personality Training												
General Business Practice												
VI. SCIENTIFIC LECTURES												
1. Sanitation sterilization and Bacteriology pertaining to Cosmetology					26	26	5½	5½	7	7		
2. Cosmetic Chemistry; Electricity; Law and Special lectures pertaining to Cosmetology												
Hygiene and Physiology; Anatomy of Hair, Skin, Nails and Muscles as pertaining to Cosmetology												
TOTAL HOURS	4	4¼	5¼		103	107	56½	60¾	89½	94¾		

FIGURE 11–2

Problems   Total the following week's activities on the appropriate time sheet. Carry the numbers over to the second sheet in their appropriate column. Then add the new weeks to the previous totals to find the new accumulated total in each problem.

1)

Date	Lecture & Theory	Hr	Demonstration	Hr	Practice	Hr	Clinic	Hr
9/7	Shampoo	¼	Shampoo	¼	Shampoo	1		
	Styling	1¼	Styling	½	Styling	1½		
			Scalp Care	¼				
9/8	Shampoo	¼	Styling	½	Shampoo	¼		
	Styling	1¼			Styling	1¾		
					Facials	1		
9/9	Rinses	¼						
	Shampoo	¾						
	Styling	½			Styling	3½		
9/10	Perm. Wave	1½	Perm. Wave	½	Perm. Wave	1½		
					Styling	1½		
9/11	Perm. Wave	1½	Perm. Wave	½	Perm. Wave	3		

FIGURE 11-3

	This Week's Hours				Theory		Demo		Practice		Clinic	
	Theory	Demo	Practice	Clinic	Balance Forward	Total	Balance Forward	Total	Balance Forward	Total	Balance Forward	Total
I. CARE OF SCALP												
Scalp care		¼			7		3 ½		14			
Shampoo	1¼	¼	1¼		6 ½		3		13¾			
Rinses	¼				4 ¼		2 ¾		9			
II. CARE OF HANDS												
Manicure— Water					11		4		20 ½			
..... Oil					4		2		7			
..... Electric												
Hand and arm bleach					1 ½		¾		2			
Hand and arm massage					1 ½		1 ¼		3			
III. CARE OF HAIR												
Hair I.												
Hairstyling and Wigs	3	1	8¼		17 ¼		8 ¾		30 ½			
Cutting, Trimming, etc.					16 ¼		8 ½		34			
Hair II.												
Permanent waves, etc.	3	1	4 ½		19 ½		9 ¾		38¾			
Or, hair pressing and marcel												
Dyes, tints, bleaches, etc.					4		2		8			
IV. CARE OF FACE												
Facial and make-up		1			7 ¼		3		15			
Special masks and packs					6 ¾		3		15			
Eyebrow arching												
V. DISPENSARY												
DESK: Shop Management					10		5		10			
Personality Training					4		2		3			
General Business Practice					6		2 ½		5 ¼			
VI. SCIENTIFIC LECTURES												
1. Sanitation sterilization and Bacteriology pertaining to Cosmetology					16 ¼		8		20			
2. Cosmetic Chemistry; Electricity; Law and Special lectures pertaining to Cosmetology												
Hygiene and Physiology; Anatomy of Hair, Skin, Nails and Muscles as pertaining to Cosmetology												
TOTAL HOURS												

FIGURE 11–4

2)

Date	Lecture & Theory	Hr	Demonstration	Hr	Practice	Hr	Clinic	Hr
11/7	Shampoo	¼	Perm. Wave	1	Perm. Wave	1 ½		
	Perm. Wave	1 ¼						
11/8	Perm. Wave	1	Perm. Wave	¾	Perm. Wave	2 ¼		
11/9	Perm. Wave	1 ½			Perm. Wave	2		
					Shampoo	¼		
					Styling	¼		
11/10	Styling	¼			Perm. Wave	1 ¾		
	Perm. Wave	1 ¼			Shampoo	¼		
					Styling	½		
11/11	Spiral Perm.	2	Spiral Perm.	1 ¼	Spiral Perm.	¾		

FIGURE 11-5

	This Week's Hours				Theory		Demo		Practice		Clinic	
	Theory	Demo	Practice	Clinic	Balance Forward	Total	Balance Forward	Total	Balance Forward	Total	Balance Forward	Total
I. CARE OF SCALP												
Scalp care					2 ¼		2 ¼		4			
Shampoo	¼		½		7		3 ½		13 ¾			
Rinses												
II. CARE OF HANDS												
Manicure— Water					6		2 ½		7			
..... Oil												
..... Electric												
Hand and arm bleach												
Hand and arm massage												
III. CARE OF HAIR												
Hair I.												
Hairstyling and Wigs	¼		¾		19		15 ½		17 ½			
Cutting, Trimming, etc.					12		6 ¼		20 ½			
Hair II.												
Permanent waves, etc.	7	3	8 ¼		11 ¼		5 ½		10 ¾			
Or, hair pressing and marcel												
Dyes, tints, bleaches, etc.												
IV. CARE OF FACE												
Facial and make-up					4		2 ½		6			
Special masks and packs												
Eyebrow arching												
V. DISPENSARY												
DESK: Shop Management					5		3		5			
Personality Training					4		½		1 ½			
General Business Practice												
VI. SCIENTIFIC LECTURES												
1. Sanitation sterilization and Bacteriology pertaining to Cosmetology												
2. Cosmetic Chemistry; Electricity; Law and Special lectures pertaining to Cosmetology												
Hygiene and Physiology; Anatomy of Hair, Skin, Nails and Muscles as pertaining to Cosmetology												
TOTAL HOURS												

FIGURE 11–6

3)

Date	Lecture & Theory	Hr	Demonstration	Hr	Practice	Hr	Clinic	Hr
1/20	Facial	1 ¼	Facial	½	Facial	½		
	Anatomy	½			Masks	½		
1/22	Anatomy	½	Facial	¼	Facial	1 ½		
	Facial	1						
1/23	Facials	1			Facial	½		
					Shampoo	½		
					Rinse	¼		
					Styling	1		
1/24	Shop Mgmt.	1 ½			Facial	½		
					Haircut	½		
					Styling	¾		

FIGURE 11-7

	THIS WEEK'S HOURS				THEORY		DEMO		PRACTICE		CLINIC	
	THEORY	DEMO	PRACTICE	CLINIC	BALANCE FORWARD	TOTAL	BALANCE FORWARD	TOTAL	BALANCE FORWARD	TOTAL	BALANCE FORWARD	TOTAL
I. CARE OF SCALP												
Scalp care					3		1 ¼		1			
Shampoo			½		5 ½		2 ½		6 ¾			
Rinses			¼		2 ¼		1		1 ½			
II. CARE OF HANDS												
Manicure— Water					1		1		1			
..... Oil												
..... Electric												
Hand and arm bleach												
Hand and arm massage												
III. CARE OF HAIR												
Hair I.												
Hairstyling and Wigs			1 ¾		17 ¼		11		13 ¾			
Cutting, Trimming, etc.					15 ½		14		18			
Hair II.												
Permanent waves, etc.					12		4		5			
Or, hair pressing and marcel												
Dyes, tints, bleaches, etc.												
IV. CARE OF FACE												
Facial and make-up	3¼	¾	3		6 ½		4 ½		7 ½			
Special masks and packs			½		1		½		½			
Eyebrow arching												
V. DISPENSARY												
DESK: Shop Management	1½				4		1 ½		6			
Personality Training												
General Business Practice												
VI. SCIENTIFIC LECTURES												
1. Sanitation sterilization and Bacteriology pertaining to Cosmetology												
2. Cosmetic Chemistry; Electricity; Law and Special lectures pertaining to Cosmetology												
Hygiene and Physiology; Anatomy of Hair, Skin, Nails and Muscles as pertaining to Cosmetology	1											
TOTAL HOURS												

FIGURE 11-8

4)

Date	Lecture & Theory	Hr	Demonstration	Hr	Practice	Hr	Clinic	Hr
3/16	Gen. Business	2	Business	½	Business	1		
					Shampoo	¼		
					Rinse	¼		
					Styling	½		
3/17	Gen. Business	1 ½	Business	1	Business	½		
					Styling	2		
3/18	Shop Mgmt.	1 ¼			Shampoo	½		
					Haircutting	2		
					Styling	¾		
3/19	Personality	1			Business	½		
					Hair styling	3		
3/20	Shop Mgmt.	½	Shop Mgmt.	1 ½	Business	½		
					Shop Mgmt.	1		
					Hair cutting	¾		
					Styling	¾		
		—		—		—		

FIGURE 11-9

	THIS WEEK'S HOURS				THEORY		DEMO		PRACTICE		CLINIC	
	THEORY	DEMO	PRACTICE	CLINIC	BALANCE FORWARD	TOTAL	BALANCE FORWARD	TOTAL	BALANCE FORWARD	TOTAL	BALANCE FORWARD	TOTAL
I. CARE OF SCALP												
Scalp care					4		1 ½		7			
Shampoo			¾		6 ½		3		10 ½			
Rinses			¼		2		1 ½		10			
II. CARE OF HANDS												
Manicure— Water					1		½		4			
..... Oil					1		1		5 ¼			
..... Electric												
Hand and arm bleach												
Hand and arm massage					1		1		3			
III. CARE OF HAIR												
Hair I.												
Hairstyling and Wigs			7		21		17		25 ¼			
Cutting, Trimming, etc.			2 ¾		14 ½		11 ¼		20 ½			
Hair II.												
Permanent waves, etc.					16		10		18			
Or, hair pressing and marcel					1		½		16			
Dyes, tints, bleaches, etc.					4		4		7			
IV. CARE OF FACE												
Facial and make-up					3		4		6 ½			
Special masks and packs					1		½		1 ½			
Eyebrow arching												
V. DISPENSARY												
DESK: Shop Management	1¾	1	1		6		5		10 ½			
Personality Training	1				1		1		3 ¼			
General Business Practice	3 ½	1½	2 ½		½		1		5 ½			
VI. SCIENTIFIC LECTURES												
1. Sanitation sterilization and Bacteriology pertaining to Cosmetology					14		10		7			
2. Cosmetic Chemistry; Electricity; Law and Special lectures pertaining to Cosmetology					9		7 ½		4			
Hygiene and Physiology; Anatomy of Hair, Skin, Nails and Muscles as pertaining to Cosmetology					14		17		2			
TOTAL HOURS												

FIGURE 11–10

5)

Date	Lecture & Theory	Hr	Demonstration	Hr	Practice	Hr	Clinic	Hr
10/10	Water Manicure	1 ½	Water Manicure	½	Water Manicure	2		
10/11	Water Manicure	1	Water Manicure	1	Water Manicure	2		
10/12	Anatomy	½	Water Manicure	¼	Water Manicure	2		
	Water Manicure	¾			Styling	½		
10/13	Sanitization	¼	Massage	¾	Massage	1 ¾		
	Anatomy	½						
	Massage	¾						
10/14	Oil Manicure	1	Oil Manicure	½	Oil Manicure	¾		
					Water Manicure	¾		
					Styling	1		
		‾‾		‾‾		‾‾		

FIGURE 11–11

	THIS WEEK'S HOURS				THEORY		DEMO		PRACTICE		CLINIC	
	THEORY	DEMO	PRACTICE	CLINIC	BALANCE FORWARD	TOTAL	BALANCE FORWARD	TOTAL	BALANCE FORWARD	TOTAL	BALANCE FORWARD	TOTAL
I. CARE OF SCALP												
Scalp care					10		3 ½		15 ¼			
Shampoo					10		4 ¾		12 ¼			
Rinses					7 ½		2 ¼		10 ½			
II. CARE OF HANDS												
Manicure— Water	3¼	1¾	6¾		1 ¾		2 ¾					
..... Oil	1	½	¾		½		½					
..... Electric												
Hand and arm bleach												
Hand and arm massage	¾	¾	1¾									
III. CARE OF HAIR												
Hair I.												
Hairstyling and Wigs			1 ½		25 ¼		7 ½		40 ¼			
Cutting, Trimming, etc.					30 ½		6 ¼		31 ¼			
Hair II.												
Permanent waves, etc.					17 ½		7 ¼		42			
Or, hair pressing and marcel												
Dyes, tints, bleaches, etc.					14 ¾		5		10			
IV. CARE OF FACE												
Facial and make-up					6 ½		4		10			
Special masks and packs					1		1		3 ½			
Eyebrow arching					3		1		1			
V. DISPENSARY												
DESK: Shop Management					4		2		1 ½			
Personality Training					5 ¼		1		1			
General Business Practice					¾		1		4 ½			
VI. SCIENTIFIC LECTURES												
1. Sanitation sterilization and Bacteriology pertaining to Cosmetology	¼				6 ½		1		7 ½			
2. Cosmetic Chemistry; Electricity; Law and Special lectures pertaining to Cosmetology												
Hygiene and Physiology; Anatomy of Hair, Skin, Nails and Muscles as pertaining to Cosmetology	1				17 ½		1		3			
TOTAL HOURS												

FIGURE 11–12

Appointment Scheduling

Another aspect of time that is important to a cosmetologist is the scheduling of appointments. An experienced cosmetologist knows that she will benefit more by having customers arrive in a timely fashion. She will not benefit if they are made to wait for long periods of time. Likewise, no benefit is gained if she is left with nothing to do for a long period of time. It requires experience to achieve this balance—a balance that keeps you busy and earning money, but not overworked and disappointing customers.

It helps to know how long each different kind of service will take and what breaks you might have during a service. For example, when giving a permanent you will have a break after the hair is rolled. This break is often long enough to give a haircut or a shampoo and set.

In Figures 11-13 to 11-18, you will find the approximate times required to give each service. These times are considered average for an experienced stylist (not a student) and they will offer a starting point from which to begin considering the process of scheduling appointments.

PERM

Procedure	Your Time	Time Waiting
Shampoo, apply pre-perm conditioner	5	10
Rinse conditioner, cut, wrap	30	20
Neutralize	5	5
Style: blow dry	20	
pick	5	
set	10	30 under dryer

FIGURE 11-13

FROST

Procedure	Your Time	Time Waiting
Pull through cap, frost	15	30
Rinse, apply toner	2	5
Set under dryer	1	40

FIGURE 11-14

BLEACH		
Procedure	Your Time	Time Waiting
Apply	5	30
Rinse, shampoo, condition	5	5
Rinse, dry	5	10
Toner application	5	30
Wash, cut, curl	35	

FIGURE 11-15

TINT		
Procedure	Your Time	Time Waiting
Apply tint	5	30
Rinse, shampoo, condition	10	
Blow dry or set	15	

FIGURE 11-16

UPDO		
Procedure	Your Time	Time Waiting
Undo other updo, wash	20	45 dry
Blow dry or set, comb out	30	

FIGURE 11-17

Procedure		Your Time
Shampoo/Set		15 min
Comb Out		15 min
Shampoo/Style		15 min
Condition Trmt.		15 min
Cut	regular customer	20 min
	new customer	30 min
	special situations	60 min

FIGURE 11-18

As you can see, most of the services that you will perform as a cosmetologist have times where you are actively involved with the client and also times where you are waiting. It is wise to take advantage of those waiting times, when they are long enough, to schedule another customer.

Scheduling appointments requires judgment on your part. Should you schedule two people at once? When should you plan a tight schedule and when should you leave extra time? Here are some hints:

- When offering a conditioning treatment at the beginning of your appointment (such as in the permanent listed in the figures, you can schedule someone else with a short appointment at the same time. Begin the conditioning with the first customer; while they are waiting begin the next person's service.)
- When you are seeing regular customers you can often schedule more tightly than when you are seeing a customer for the first time. It takes a new customer longer to express to you what they would like to have done.
- When you are cutting very long hair for someone allow more time than usual. This is necessary because it is wise to cut their hair in stages—a little at a time—to avoid the disatisfaction that can often accompany a sudden change in hair styles.
- When in doubt, schedule your appointments loosely. Although it is to your advantage to earn as much money as you can in your working hours, you don't want to make customers wait.

To schedule appointments be sure that you have enough time (or nearly enough) to complete the scheduled services between breaks in another customer's service or before another customer arrives.

Example 1:   Schedule the following appointments in the earliest available time slot: a perm w/ blow dry, a hair cut, an updo, and a frost.

1) Be aware that appointments are generally given over the phone or as a customer is leaving his current appointment. Once the time is given to them you do not want to re-arrange the appointment. In this text schedule the services as they are listed, assuming that that is the order that the customers requested their appointments.

2)

	DATE	
		00
		10
	8	20
		30
		40
		50
Perm Haircut		00
		10
	9	20
		30
		40
		50
		00
		10
	10	20
Updo		30
		40
		50
Frost		00
		10
	11	20
		30
		40
		50
		00
		10
	12	20
		30
		40
		50

FIGURE 11-19

3) The perm is scheduled at 9:00 when the shop opens. While the pre-permanent conditioning is setting, you could begin the haircut. This should also be scheduled at 9:00 (and begun as soon as possible after beginning the conditioning). The updo can begin as soon as the permanent is finished which would be 10:35. You should schedule the updo at 10:30 (on an even $\frac{1}{4}$ hour interval) and begin her as soon as possible. The frost could begin while the updo is sitting under the dryer (after 20 minutes spent in washing and setting hair). This should be scheduled at 11:00 (again on the $\frac{1}{4}$ hour interval). You may have to interrupt the comb-out of the updo to rinse the frost customer and apply toner and then to set them under the dryer, but these would be short interruptions which are common in a salon.

Problems   Schedule the following appointments at the earliest times available. Keep them in the order that the appointments were requested (with the exception of scheduling short services such as cuts and shampoo/sets into the breaks available in the longer services). Schedule all appointments on even $\frac{1}{4}$ hour intervals.

1) Schedule the following: a perm with blow dry, a perm with set, an updo, a shampoo/set, a hair cut, a hair cut, a frost, and a frost.

	DATE	
		00
		10
		20
	8	30
		40
		50
		00
		10
		20
	9	30
		40
		50
		00
		10
		20
	10	30
		40
		50
		00
		10
		20
	11	30
		40
		50
		00
		10
		20
	12	30
		40
		50

FIGURE 11-20

2) Schedule the following: a hair cut, a tint, a shampoo/set, a perm with blow dry, a perm with blow dry, a hair cut, a frost, and a hair cut.

	DATE	
		00
		10
		20
	8	30
		40
		50
		00
		10
		20
	9	30
		40
		50
		00
		10
		20
	10	30
		40
		50
		00
		10
		20
	11	30
		40
		50
		00
		10
		20
	12	30
		40
		50

FIGURE 11-20

3) Schedule the following: a bleach, a tint, a perm with blow dry, an updo, a shampoo/set, an updo, an updo, a shampoo/set, and a hair cut.

	DATE	
	8	00
		10
		20
		30
		40
		50
	9	00
		10
		20
		30
		40
		50
	10	00
		10
		20
		30
		40
		50
	11	00
		10
		20
		30
		40
		50
	12	00
		10
		20
		30
		40
		50

FIGURE 11-20

4) Schedule the following: a perm with set, a hair cut, a hair cut, a frost, a tint, a bleach, a perm with blow dry, an updo, a shampoo/set, and a hair cut.

	DATE	
	8	00
		10
		20
		30
		40
		50
	9	00
		10
		20
		30
		40
		50
	10	00
		10
		20
		30
		40
		50
	11	00
		10
		20
		30
		40
		50
	12	00
		10
		20
		30
		40
		50

FIGURE 11-20

5) Schedule the following: a hair cut, a hair cut, a hair cut, a perm with blow dry, a bleach, an updo, a shampoo/set, and and perm with set.

	DATE	
		00
		10
		20
	8	30
		40
		50
		00
		10
		20
	9	30
		40
		50
		00
		10
		20
	10	30
		40
		50
		00
		10
		20
	11	30
		40
		50
		00
		10
		20
	12	30
		40
		50

FIGURE 11-20

Chapter 12

Income

Gross Pay

Gross pay is the amount of pay earned for a given period of time. Common time periods used for payment are weekly, monthly, biweekly, and semimonthly. Those who are paid weekly receive a check 52 times a year. Those who are paid monthly receive a check 12 times a year. Biweekly means every 2 weeks (or every other week on the same day of the week—i.e. every other Friday) and therefore occurs 26 times a year. Semimonthly means every half a month (twice a month on designated dates—i.e. the 1st and 15th or each month) and therefore occurs 24 times a year.

The type of job you have determines how your pay will be computed. In cosmetology, pay is most often computed by commission—that is, receiving a certain percentage of the price of the service performed. Occasionally a cosmetologist might receive hourly pay. This is true especially of individuals who stay in a field related to cosmetology but do not work as a cosmetologist—sales representatives, managers, receptionists, etc. This section will show examples of situations where hourly pay might be considered.

Commission

To figure commission multiply the rate of commission (the percent you are to receive) by the price of the service performed. Remember that to multiply by a percent, it is necessary to change the percent to a decimal first (by moving the decimal two places to the left.)

Example 1: Kris receives 35% commission on all services she performs at Faylor's Beauty Salon. This past week she completed $895 worth of services. Find her gross pay.

$$
\begin{array}{r}
895.00 \\
\times \quad .35 \\
\hline
447500 \\
268500 \\
\hline
313.2500 = \$313.25
\end{array}
$$

Hourly Pay

To figure straight time multiply the regular hours worked by the pay received per hour.

Example 1: June worked 37 hours and earns $4.29 per hour. Compute her gross pay.

$4.29 \times 37 = \$158.73$

Overtime pay is either computed at time and a half (one and a half times as much money per hour) or double time (twice as much per hour). To figure overtime pay multiply the pay received per hour by either 1.5 (for time and a half) or 2 (for double time). Then multiply that amount per hour by the number of overtime hours worked.

Example 2: Randall worked 40 regular hours and 6 hours overtime. His manager pays overtime at time and a half. He earns $6.92 per hour. Find his straight time pay, his overtime pay, and his total pay.

Straight time

$$\begin{array}{r} \$ \quad 6.92 \\ \times \quad \underline{40} \text{ hours} \\ \$ \ 276.80 \end{array}$$

Overtime

$$\begin{array}{r} \$ \ 6.92 \\ \times \quad \underline{1.5} \text{ time and a half} \\ \$10.38 \text{ per hour for overtime} \\ \times \quad \underline{6} \text{ hours overtime} \\ \$62.28 \end{array}$$

$276.80 + $62.28 = $ 339.08 total pay

Salary

To figure gross pay for an individual who earns a salary (a fixed amount per year regardless of hours worked), divide the salary amount by how many pay periods are in one year. For example, if they are paid weekly you would divide by 52; biweekly, 26; monthly, 12; and semimonthly, 24.

Example 1: Jack Reams earns $27,590 per year as a product consultant for Maxavelle cosmetics. He is paid biweekly. What is his gross pay?

biweekly = 26 $26\overline{)27{,}590.}$ 1,061.153 Use thousandths place to decide how to round.

Gross Pay is $1,061.15

Problems   Determine each individual's gross pay.

1) Jerome Byler works at NuLife Creations. He earns 42% commission. His sales last week were $1,010. What is his gross pay? _____

2) Jessica Todd owns Jessica's. She pays herself a weekly check based on 55% commission. Last week her services totalled $1,243. What is her gross pay? _____

3) Lisa Bonatelli works at Out Back Salon. She earns 36% commission. Her sales last week totalled $610. What is her gross pay? _____

4) Carrie is a stylist at Hair Happenings in the Village Mall. She earns 52% commission. Her services last week totalled $996.50. What is her gross pay? _____

5) Agnes Flores is a manicurist at Top of the Toes Salon. She earns 60% commission. Her services last week totalled $512. What is her gross pay? _____

6) Jeffrey Togassi works at Fremont Hair Hut. He earns 48% commission. His services last month totalled $1,875.50. What is his gross pay for the month? _____

7) Karen Wheeler works at Den of Style. She earns 50% commission. Her services last week totalled $772.75. What is her gross pay? _____

8) Brett Petersen works at Castle Hair Center. He earns 44% commission. His services last week totalled $508. What is his gross pay?   _____

9) Clark Robinson is a salesman for San Pedro Beauty Supply Company. He earns 35% commission on all of his first time sales and 31% commission on continuing orders. What is his gross pay in a week where he had $835 in new sales and $651.78 in continuing sales?   _____

10) Deloris Carmel is an image consultant for Career Directions. She receives 65% commission on all consultations she completes. Her services for the month of August totalled $2,753.50. What is her gross pay?   _____

11) RaeAnn works as a receptionist for a large salon and earns $5.71 per hour. What is her gross pay for a week in which she worked 38.5 hours?   _____

12) Dean earns $12.89 per hour as a manager of a beauty supply store. What is his gross pay for a week in which he worked 40 hours?   _____

13) Justine works $37\frac{3}{4}$ hours a week as a teacher's assistant at a school of cosmetology. She earns $8.10 per hour. What is her gross pay for the week?   _____

14) Jeff works at Fanfare Total Look Salon as a manicurist. What is his gross pay for a week in which he works 25 hours and earns $6.45 per hour?   _____

15) Laura Montgomery works as a cosmetologist in a care center for the elderly. She earns $11.21 per hour and earns time and a half for overtime. What is her gross pay for a week in which she works 40 regular hours and $6\frac{1}{2}$ hours overtime?   _____

16) Rick earns $5.37 per hour as a laboratory assistant at EuroWave Beauty Products. What is his gross pay in a week in which he works $41\frac{1}{4}$ regular hours?   _____

17) Carol works at Hair Care Centre as a skin care consultant. She earns $6.40 per hour and gets double time for overtime. What is her pay for the week in which she works 40 regular hours and $7\frac{1}{2}$ overtime hours?   _____

18) Darla earns $11.90 per hour as an institutional cosmetologist. She worked 30 regular hours last week. Find her gross pay.   _____

19) Shannon works at Beauty Supplies, Inc. as a researcher. She earns $10.88 per hour and double time for overtime. What is her pay for a week in which she works 40 regular hours and 7 overtime hours?   _____

20) Leslie Wireman works for NewLooks, Inc. as an image consultant. She is paid $7.01 per hour and earns time and a half for overtime on Saturday and double time for overtime on Sunday. What is her pay for a week in which she worked 40 regular hours, 6 hours on Saturday, and 4 hours on Sunday?   _____

21) Joan earns $14,975 a year as a manager at a fitness spa. What is her gross pay each week? _____

22) Scott earns $21,807 a year as a model for Gabriel Products. What is his bi-weekly gross pay? _____

23) Wayne gets paid once a month in his job as a advertising agent for Gabriel Products. What is his monthly gross pay if he earns $36,496 a year? _____

24) Jill earns $20,411 a year as a cosmetology instructor. What is her semi-monthly pay? _____

25) Rick is a barber at Day View Nursing Home. He earns $4.90 per hour. What is his weekly pay for a week in which he works $37\frac{1}{2}$ regular hours? _____

26) Match the following pay periods with the correct description:

PAY DAY(S)	DESCRIPTION	# OF PERIODS
a. the 5th of every month	_____ biweekly	_____ 24
b. every Tuesday	_____ monthly	_____ 52
c. the 10th and 25th of every month	_____ weekly	_____ 12
d. every other Friday	_____ semi-monthly	_____ 26

Deductions

Federal Income Tax

Federal Income Tax is deducted from each paycheck based on your marital status, your income, and how many allowances you claim.

An allowance is a credit for each person you financially support (yourself, your spouse, children, older parents, etc.). You may claim as many people as you support but you are not required to claim all of them.

- If you claim all allowances, less will be deducted from each paycheck. However, you probably will not get a very large tax refund at the end of the year and you may even have to pay.

- If you claim less allowances, more will be deducted from each paycheck. This will probably "store up" enough with the government that you will get a larger refund. Some individuals see this as a way to save money for a special purpose.

The amount deducted from an individual's paycheck is determined by reading a table. There is a separate table for singles and for those who are married. A single person has more deducted per week than a married person with the same income and allowances.

WEEKLY PAYROLL DEDUCTION FOR FIT FOR MARRIED PERSONS

The wages are		The withholding allowances are						
At least	But less than	0	1	2	3	4	5	6
200	210	21.08	18.12	15.07	12.15	9.07	6.17	3.07
210	220	22.04	19.06	16.03	13.08	10.06	7.02	4.06
220	230	22.97	20.01	16.95	14.08	10.98	8.05	4.98
230	240	23.88	20.75	17.88	14.74	11.83	8.79	5.83
240	250	24.75	21.01	18.75	15.05	12.79	9.04	6.79
250	260	25.61	22.17	19.62	16.12	13.64	10.14	7.64
260	270	26.82	23.64	20.83	17.68	14.85	11.67	8.85
270	280	27.50	24.25	21.58	18.23	15.52	12.22	9.52
280	290	29.00	25.73	23.05	19.76	17.01	13.78	11.01
290	300	30.63	26.99	24.68	20.91	18.64	14.94	12.64
300	310	31.98	27.50	25.93	21.58	19.98	15.50	13.98
310	320	33.14	29.95	27.16	23.93	21.19	17.92	15.19
320	330	34.78	30.78	28.77	24.70	22.75	18.75	16.75
330	340	36.22	32.77	30.23	26.76	24.26	20.76	18.26
340	350	37.76	34.54	31.77	28.54	25.73	22.59	19.73
350	360	39.05	35.17	33.09	29.18	27.09	23.14	21.09
360	370	40.44	37.80	34.47	31.83	28.44	25.89	22.44
370	380	41.70	38.27	35.79	32.27	29.70	26.24	23.70
380	390	42.93	39.00	36.95	33.04	30.90	27.07	24.90
390	400	44.21	40.85	38.26	34.89	32.25	28.89	26.25

WEEKLY PAYROLL DEDUCTION FOR FIT FOR SINGLE PERSONS

The wages are		The withholding allowances are						
At least	But less than	0	1	2	3	4	5	6
200	210	24.04	21.14	18.07	15.14	12.03	9.12	6.05
210	220	25.04	22.08	19.03	16.07	13.04	10.03	7.08
220	230	25.97	23.05	19.95	17.05	13.97	11.06	7.93
230	240	26.84	23.79	20.88	17.79	14.82	11.78	8.88
240	250	27.72	24.02	21.75	18.03	15.79	12.04	9.74
250	260	28.67	25.14	22.62	19.15	16.60	13.19	10.65
260	270	29.84	26.65	23.83	20.62	17.86	14.60	11.88
270	280	30.59	27.27	24.58	21.21	18.59	15.24	12.53
280	290	31.05	28.70	26.05	22.74	20.08	16.78	14.05
290	300	33.64	29.97	27.68	23.98	21.63	17.92	15.68
300	310	34.98	30.59	28.93	24.50	22.95	18.52	16.99
310	320	36.12	32.94	30.16	26.95	24.12	20.96	18.12
320	330	37.79	33.75	31.77	27.76	25.71	21.71	19.75
330	340	39.24	35.77	33.23	29.79	26.27	23.77	21.22
340	350	40.74	37.53	34.77	31.53	28.74	25.55	22.79
350	360	42.05	38.19	36.09	32.19	30.09	26.19	24.00
360	370	43.48	39.86	37.47	34.85	31.40	28.83	25.44
370	380	44.72	41.29	38.79	35.28	32.77	29.29	26.76
380	390	45.99	42.08	39.95	36.04	33.99	30.04	27.92
390	400	47.20	43.84	41.26	37.89	35.24	31.88	29.28

To determine FIT withheld:

1. Choose the appropriate table for marital status.
2. Look for the row which includes the income amount (the amount <u>must</u> be weekly income).
3. Read over to the appropriate number of allowances.
4. The amount from the table is the FIT withheld.

Problems   Find each individual's FIT withheld.

		Marital Status	Allowances	Weekly Income	FIT Withheld
1)	Joe Belaquin	M	2	$ 211.80	_____
2)	Jane Milligan	M	1	$ 388.16	_____
3)	Laura Hillshire	S	0	$ 270.00	_____
4)	Sarina Green	M	4	$ 241.87	_____
5)	Rico Gomez	S	0	$ 349.99	_____
6)	Allen Silvers	M	3	$ 353.44	_____
7)	Carla Pennington	S	1	$ 274.16	_____
8)	Bob Dome	S	1	$ 202.08	_____
9)	JaShonda Michaels	S	0	$ 330.00	_____
10)	Ray Everett	M	4	$ 376.55	_____

11) Coretta Shields earned $271.49 this week as a barber. She is divorced and claims 3 allowances. What is her FIT withheld?   _____

12) Troy Blake is married and supports his wife and three children. He claims all of the allowances he is entitled to claim.

    a. How many allowances does he claim?   _____

    b. How much FIT is withheld if he earns $380.00 per week?   _____

13) Jennifer Carpenter recently got married. When she was single she claimed 1 allowance. Now that she is married she will claim zero to maintain approximately the same deduction amount. Her weekly income is $245.48.

    a. What was the amount of FIT withheld when she was single?   _____

    b. What is her FIT withheld now that she is married?   _____

14) Duane Shearer earns $18,200 a year as an manager at Moland Beauty Supply. He is married and claims 3 allowances. What is his FIT withheld?   _____

15) Vanessa Beauve' operates a cosmetics store. She earns $20,277.40 a year. She is single and claims zero allowances. What is her FIT withheld?   _____

State Income Tax

State Income Tax is deducted from each paycheck based on your marital status, your income, and how many dependents you have.

For each person you support you receive an exemption on your state taxes. An exemption is a credit for each person you financially support (yourself, your spouse, children, older parents, etc.) The table below shows an example of the exemptions a state might allow.

PERSONAL EXEMPTIONS	
Single	$ 2,000
Married	4,000
Each dependent	1,000

This amount is deducted from your annual income to determine your taxable income. Taxable income is then multiplied by the state tax rate to determine annual state tax.

Example 1: Jeff Reed earns $14,500 a year as an cosmetology instructor. He is married and has 1 dependent. His state has a $2\frac{1}{2}$% tax rate. Find the annual state tax.

1) Find taxable income. (Annual income − exemptions)

$14,500 − 4,000 − 1,000 = $9,500
            married   dependent

2) Find annual state tax. (Taxable income x rate)

$ 9,500 × 2.5% = $237.50

Problems Find each individual's state income tax withheld. Use the table provided for exemptions.

	State Tax Rate	Marital Status	Dependents	Annual Income	Annual State Tax
1) D. Bryan	2.5%	M	2	$ 7,900	_____
2) S. Evans	4.1%	S	0	$11,250	_____
3) C. Carr	3.75%	S	1	$14,115	_____
4) S. Hale	5%	M	4	$26,630	_____
5) R. Callas	4.25%	S	1	$20,050	_____
6) P. Reese	3%	M	3	$16,800	_____
7) J. Cole	3.2%	M	1	$18,000	_____
8) L. Wheeler	4.25%	S	0	$19,135	_____
9) J. Juarez	4%	M	2	$15,885	_____
10) A. Blair	2%	S	1	$11,488	_____

11) Sheree Cabon works at Cut Above Hair Salons, Inc. as a public relations manager. She earns $561.00 a week. She is married and has 2 dependents. Her state has a $1\frac{1}{2}\%$ tax rate.

  a. Find her annual salary. _____

  b. Find her annual state tax withheld. _____

12) Joy Petrie earns $5.22 per hour as a receptionist at Tans Unlimited. She works 40 hours a week, 52 weeks a year. She is single and has 0 dependents. Her state tax rate is 4.24%.

  a. Find her annual salary. _____

  b. Find her annual state tax withheld. _____

13) Angela Windela earns $18,788 a year as a manager at Dillon's Salon. She is single and has no dependents. Her state tax rate is 2.75%.

  a. Find her annual state tax withheld. _____

  b. Find the amount withheld from each paycheck is she is paid semi-monthly. _____

14) Ray Bolson earns $189.88 weekly as a beautician at Daystar Nursing Care Center. He is single and has 1 dependent. His state tax rate is 4%.

  a. Find his annual salary. _____

  b. Find his annual state tax withheld. _____

  c. Find his weekly state tax withheld. _____

15) Renee Waycliffe is a demonstrator for ColorAnalysis Cosmetics. She is married and has 4 dependents. She earns $1115.89 monthly. Her state tax rate is 6.2%.

  a. Find her annual salary. _____

  b. Find her annual state tax withheld. _____

  c. Find her weekly state tax withheld. _____

FICA Tax (Social Security Tax)

Federal Insurance Contributions Act (FICA) tax is deducted from each paycheck at a rate of 7.65% up to a total earning of $45,000 a year. After $45,000 has been earned by the individual, they no longer pay social security tax that year. They begin paying it again at the beginning of the next year.

  To compute FICA tax it is important to first determine whether the individual has earned over $45,000 so far during the year. If so, FICA tax withheld will be zero for that pay period and all others remaining that year.

  If they have not yet earned $45,000, FICA is found by multiplying their gross pay for the pay period by 7.65%.

Example 1:   Janet Slade earns $286 per week as a cosmetologist. She has earned $11,219 so far this year. What is her FICA tax withheld?

1) Has she earned over $45,000? No, she has only earned $11,219.

2) Find FICA tax withheld. $286 × 7.65% = $21.48

Problems   Find each individual's FICA tax. The tax rate is 7.65% of the first $45,000 earned.

		Earnings So Far This year	Current Gross Pay	FICA Tax/ Pay Period
1)	Dustin Rice	$38,215	$1,060	_____
2)	Steve Houston	15,146	349	_____
3)	Alica Meyer	14,978	1,215	_____
4)	Karen Bitler	45,810	2,614	_____
5)	Sheila Cooper	27,060	419	_____
6)	Candy Craig	11,015	216	_____
7)	Summer Hayes	41,263	2,117	_____
8)	Jack Tobias	17,651	396	_____
9)	Reagan Wise	1,214	1,214	_____
10)	Cora Tyler	10,054	391	_____

11) Cliff Steiner earns $614.89 per week as a cosmetologist. He has worked 39 weeks so far this year. What will be the FICA tax withheld during his 40th week of work?   _____

12) Janice Keith earns $4,298 per month as a product analyst for McComber-O'Neill Laboratories. What will be the FICA tax withheld during December?   _____

13) Kristin Russell earns $218.90 per week as a receptionist in Get Set Salon. She has earned $10,945 so far this year. What will be her FICA tax withheld this week?   _____

14) Sharon Dailey earns $9.57 per hour as a cosmetologist at Oakland Day Care Center. She works 40 hours a week. She has earned $4593.60 so far this year. What will be her FICA tax withheld this week?   _____

15) Dale Bishop earns $16.95 per hour as a manager for Beauty Laboratories. He works a 40-hour week. He has worked 50 weeks so far this year. What will be his FICA tax withheld during his 51st week of work?   _____

Voluntary Deductions

Other deductions which may be taken out of your paycheck include medical or life insurance, credit union deductions, union dues, charitable contributions, or other work-related memberships or expenses.

Insurance deductions vary depending on whether or not they are offered by your employer as a benefit. Often an employer will agree to pay part of your insurance cost as a benefit to you while the remaining amount is deducted from your paycheck. The other voluntary deductions listed are usually taken from your check as a matter of choice and can vary in amount or frequency.

To find the amount deducted for group insurance, first find the percent of the cost that the employee must pay. You will usually be given the percent that the employer pays and you will use that information to determine what is left for the employee to pay. For example, if the employee pays 80% of the cost, that leaves 20% left for the employee to pay. (100% − 80% = 20%)

Next, multiply the percent left for the employee to pay by the annual cost of the insurance. This will give you the amount that the employee pays annually for insurance.

Finally, divide that annual amount by how many pay periods the employee works in a year. This will determine the amount deducted from their paycheck each pay period.

Example 1:   Brenda Pope has medical and life insurance through her employer. The cost of the medical insurance is $1590 per year and her employe pays 80%. The cost of the life insurance is $480 per year and her employer pays 90%. How much is deducted from her biweekly paycheck for medical and life insurance?

$$\text{Medical} = \$1590 \times 20\% \ (100\% - 80\%) = \$\,318.00$$
$$\text{Life} \quad = 480 \times 10\% \ (100\% - 90\%) \quad = \underline{\quad 48.00}$$
$$\$\,366.00 \text{ annual amount}$$

$366 divided by 26 (biweekly) = $14.08 deducted biweekly for insurance

Problems   Determine how much is deducted from each paycheck for various insurances and other voluntary deductions.

1) Jay Brianco works at Greengold Beauty Equipment as a sales representative. He has medical, life, dental, and vision insurance. He also has $15 per week deducted for union dues and $50 per week deducted to save in the credit union. His employer pays 70% of dental and vision and 90% of medical and life insurance. The annual costs are $1880 for medical, $1290 for life, $586 for dental, and $612 for vision.

a. How much is deducted each week for medical insurance?   _____

b. How much is deducted each week for life insurance?   _____

c. How much is deducted each week for dental insurance?   _____

d. How much is deducted each week for vision insurance?   _____

e. What are the total voluntary deductions?   _____

2) Chris Wheeler works at Princeville Vocational School as a cosmetology instructor. She earns $27,826 a year. She has medical and life insurance. She also has $10 deducted biweekly for the United Way. Medical insurance costs $1900 per year and life insurance costs $1480 per year. Her employer pays 85% of all insurance costs.

   a. How much is deducted biweekly for medical insurance? _____

   b. How much is deducted biweekly for life insurance? _____

   c. What are the total voluntary deductions? _____

3) Cathy Joseph is a receptionist at Hathomore's Beauty Shop. She earns $20,050 a year and is paid monthly. Her benefits include 90% coverage on medical and life insurance and 50% coverage on any other insurance plans. She has medical insurance which costs $2,098 a year, life which costs $1298 a year, vision for $950 a year, and a prescription drug card for $1105 per year.

   a. How much is deducted each month for medical insurance? _____

   b. How much is deducted each month for life insurance? _____

   c. How much is deducted each month for vision insurance? _____

   d. How much is deducted each month for prescription insurance? _____

   e. What are the total voluntary deductions? _____

4) Sherry Regent is a manicurist at Dayton Nursing Center. She has $50 a week deducted to deposit in her credit union, $5.50 a week deducted for union dues, $12.50 a week deducted for uniform fees, and $7.80 a week deducted for meals. She also has medical insurance for $16.58 a week and life for $3.21 a week. What are the total voluntary deductions? _____

5) Marie Hawkins is a fashion and beauty reporter for the Loma News. She earns $14,083 a year. She has medical insurance, life insurance, and travel insurance. She also has $10 deducted per week for deposit in her credit union. Medical insurance costs $1900 a year, life insurance costs $960 a year, and travel insurance costs $450 a year. Loma News pays 80% of all insurance.

   a. How much is deducted each week for medical insurance? _____

   b. How much is deducted each week for life insurance? _____

   c. How much is deducted each week for travel insurance? _____

   d. What are the total voluntary deductions? _____

6) Leigh Waxaw is a cosmetologist. She has medical insurance through Parkview Valley Mall's group plan. The cost of the insurance is $1926 a year, of which she pays 100%. How much does she pay each month for medical insurance? _____

7) Dana Sindell is a cosmetology illustrator for Dove Publishers. She earns $28,717 a year. She has $25 per pay period deducted for a credit union loan, $6.95 per pay period deducted for membership fees, and $5 per pay period deducted for a flower fund. What is the total of her voluntary deductions each pay period? _____

8) Donna Watson is a receptionist at New Look Fitness Salon. She has medical insurance for $1815 a year and a prescription drug card for $1224 a year through her employer. The salon pays 90% of all insurances.

   a. How much is deducted each week for medical insurance? _____

   b. How much is deducted each week for prescription insurance? _____

9) Lois Callahan works at Radel-Dowell Corp. as an image consultant. She has medical, life, dental, and vision insurance. She also has $15 per week deducted for union dues and $50 per week deducted to save in the credit union. Her employer pays 70% of the dental and vision costs and 90% of medical and life insurance costs. The annual costs are $2100 for medical, $965 for life, $495 for dental, and $705 for vision.

   a. How much is deducted each week for medical insurance? _____

   b. How much is deducted each week for life insurance? _____

   c. How much is deducted each week for dental insurance? _____

   d. How much is deducted each week for vision insurance? _____

   e. What are the total voluntary deductions? _____

10) Randy Murphy is a barber at Jefferson Nursing Home. He has $25/week deducted to deposit in his credit union, $4/week for union dues, $10.75/week for uniform fees, and $9.50/ week for meals. He also has medical insurance for $21.15/week and life for $4.55/week.

   a. What are the total voluntary deductions? _____

Net Pay

Net pay is the amount of pay earned for a given period of time after all deductions for taxes, insurances, and other voluntary deductions have been taken out. Net pay is the amount you receive in your paycheck.

   To compute net pay first find the individual's gross pay for the pay period. Next, find the sum of all deductions. Then:

GROSS PAY − DEDUCTIONS = NET PAY

Problems   Use the tables on p. 126 for FIT and find each individual's net pay.

1) Anna Deskart earns $6.08 per hour and double time for all overtime. Last week she worked 40 regular hours and 4 overtime hours. She is single, has 1 dependent, and claims two allowances. Her state tax rate is 4.05%. She has earned $10,496 so far this year.

   a. Find her gross pay for the week.   _____

   b. Find her FIT withheld for the week.   _____

   c. Find her state tax withheld last week.   _____

   d. Find her FICA tax withheld last week.   _____

   e. Find the total of all deductions.   _____

   f. Find her net pay.   _____

2) Phil Everly earns $25,208 a year as a beauty salon chain executive. He gets paid weekly. He is married, has 3 dependents, and claims 0 allowances. His state tax rate is 2.5%. He has $15 per week deducted for deposit in his credit union and $2 per week deducted for membership dues.

   a. Find his gross pay for the week.   _____

   b. Find his FIT withheld for the week.   _____

   c. Find his state tax withheld per week.   _____

   d. Find his FICA tax withheld per week.   _____

   e. Find the total of all deductions.   _____

   f. Find his net pay.   _____

3) Cecil Mosgrove works on the assembly line at New Life Beauty Supply and earns $5.70 per hour. He works 40 hours a week. He is married, has two children, and claims 4 allowances. His state tax rate is 4% and he has worked 27 weeks so far this year. He has $2.80 deducted per week for union dues.

   a. Find his gross pay for the week.   _____

   b. Find his FIT withheld for the week.   _____

   c. How much has he earned so far this year?   _____

   d. Find his state tax withheld per week.   _____

   e. Find his FICA tax withheld per week.   _____

   f. Find the total of all deductions.   _____

   g. Find his net pay.   _____

4) Jana Wyler earns $31,826 a year as a cosmetology instructor at Highland Technical School. She is married with no dependents. She claims no allowances. Her state does not assess a tax.

a. Find her gross pay for the week.   _____

b. Find her FIT withheld for the week.   _____

c. Find her state tax withheld per week.   _____

d. Find her FICA tax withheld per week.   _____

e. Find the total of all deductions.   _____

f. Find her net pay.   _____

5) Audrey Banks works as a manicurist at Ashville Hills Elderly Care Center. She earns $5.25 per hour and works 40 hours a week. She is single with no dependents and claims 0 allowances. Her state tax rate is 5.25%.

a. Find her gross pay for the week.   _____

b. Find her FIT withheld for the week.   _____

c. Find her state tax withheld per week.   _____

d. Find her FICA tax withheld per week.   _____

e. Find the total of all deductions.   _____

f. Find her net pay.   _____

Earning Statement

An earning statement is a record of an employee's earnings, deductions, and net pay. Often they also contain a record of the individual's earnings and deductions so far during the year (earnings to date).

The earning statement is often attached to the individual's paycheck and is sometimes called a check stub. The earning statement and the paycheck itself can be done by hand, by computer, or on a write-it-once system like Control-O-Fax.

Problems   Complete the following earning statements using the problems solved in the previous section of this workbook (Net Pay — problems #1–#5)

1) Employee: Anna Deskart
   S.S.#:   211-41-8112

NAME			S.S. #		PAY RATE	
FIT	FICA		STATE	OTHER		TOTAL DED.
REG. PAY	OVERTIME PAY		GROSS PAY		NET PAY	

FIGURE 12-1

2) Employee: Phil Everly
   S.S.#:   196-06-8621

Name		S.S. #		Pay Rate	
FIT	FICA	State	Other	Total Ded.	
Reg. Pay	Overtime Pay	Gross Pay		Net Pay	

FIGURE 12-1

3) Employee: Cecil Mosgrove
   S.S.#:   313-13-3113

Name_____   Reg. Pay_____

S.S.#_____   Overtime Pay_____

Pay Rate_____

THIS PAY PERIOD   YEAR TO DATE

Gross Pay_____   Gross Pay_____

FIT_____   FIT_____

State_____   State_____

FICA_____   FICA_____

Other_____   Other_____

Net Pay_____   Net Pay_____

4) Employee: Jana Wyler
   S.S.#:   276-01-0455

Name		S.S. #		Pay Rate	
FIT	FICA	State	Other	Total Ded.	
Reg. Pay	Overtime Pay	Gross Pay		Net Pay	

FIGURE 12-1

5) Employee: Audrey Banks
   S.S.#:   416-00-5523

NAME		S.S. #		PAY RATE
FIT	FICA	STATE	OTHER	TOTAL DED.
REG. PAY	OVERTIME PAY	GROSS PAY	NET PAY	

FIGURE 12-1

Paychecks

To write a paycheck most offices or companies use an official payroll check rather than one from their normal checking account. It is necessary to have an authorized signature on all checks written. Sometimes the one completing the payroll is given the authority to sign the checks and other times an owner, office manager, or other supervisor may sign the checks. In these exercises you have the authority to sign the checks.

To complete a check, fill in the date it is being written, the name of the employee, the amount of net pay in numbers and also in words (as explained in Chapter 1). Then sign the check. If an earning statement is attached, complete it as well.

Problems   Complete a paycheck for each employee in the previous section.

1)

TOTAL LOOK BEAUTY SALON   CHECK NO. **1266**
1362 SUTTON DRIVE EAST   3523-411
BRANDON, IL 57233   3755

                            Date _____
PAY TO THE
ORDER OF _____ $ [   ]

_____ DOLLARS

    FOSBERG BANK, NA
       BRANDON, IL
                            _____
  5723362-7704-67-1266

FIGURE 12-2

2)

TOTAL LOOK BEAUTY SALON   CHECK NO. **1266**
1362 SUTTON DRIVE EAST   3523-411
BRANDON, IL 57233   3755

                            Date _____
PAY TO THE
ORDER OF _____ $ [   ]

_____ DOLLARS

    FOSBERG BANK, NA
       BRANDON, IL
                            _____
  5723362-7704-67-1266

FIGURE 12-2

3)

TOTAL LOOK BEAUTY SALON
1362 SUTTON DRIVE EAST
BRANDON, IL 57233

CHECK NO. **1266**

$\dfrac{3523-411}{3755}$

DATE _____

PAY TO THE
ORDER OF _____ $ _____

_____ DOLLARS

FOSBERG BANK, NA
BRANDON, IL

_____

5724362-7704567-1266

FIGURE 12-2

4)

TOTAL LOOK BEAUTY SALON
1362 SUTTON DRIVE EAST
BRANDON, IL 57233

CHECK NO. **1266**

$\dfrac{3523-411}{3755}$

DATE _____

PAY TO THE
ORDER OF _____ $ _____

_____ DOLLARS

FOSBERG BANK, NA
BRANDON, IL

_____

5724362-7704567-1266

FIGURE 12-2

5)

TOTAL LOOK BEAUTY SALON
1362 SUTTON DRIVE EAST
BRANDON, IL 57233

CHECK NO. **1266**

$\dfrac{3523-411}{3755}$

DATE _____

PAY TO THE
ORDER OF _____ $ _____

_____ DOLLARS

FOSBERG BANK, NA
BRANDON, IL

_____

5724362-7704567-1266

FIGURE 12-2

In problems #6–#10 complete each week's earning statement and paycheck for George Prang. (S.S. #: 017–17–2416) He is married, has 3 children, and claims all allowances he is entitled to claim. His state tax rate is $2\frac{3}{4}$% with no exemptions allowed. He has earned $18,106 so far this year. He earns $7.80 an hour with time and a half for overtime.

6) George worked 40 regular hours and 6 hours overtime. He has $22.01 deducted this week for health insurance and $25.00 deducted for union dues.

Name		S.S. #		Pay Rate	
FIT	FICA	State	Other	Total Ded.	
Reg. Pay	Overtime Pay	Gross Pay		Net Pay	

FIGURE 12–1

TotaL Look Beauty Salon
1362 Sutton Drive East
Brandon, IL 57233

Check No. **1266**
3523–411
3755

Date _____

Pay to the
Order of _____ $ _____

_____ Dollars

Fosberg Bank, NA
Brandon, IL

572436277046712266

FIGURE 12–2

7) George worked 40 regular hours and $3\frac{1}{2}$ hours overtime.

Name		S.S. #		Pay Rate	
FIT	FICA	State	Other	Total Ded.	
Reg. Pay	Overtime Pay	Gross Pay		Net Pay	

FIGURE 12–1

TotaL Look Beauty Salon
1362 Sutton Drive East
Brandon, IL 57233

Check No. **1266**
3523–411
3755

Date _____

Pay to the
Order of _____ $ _____

_____ Dollars

Fosberg Bank, NA
Brandon, IL

572436277046712266

FIGURE 12–2

8) George worked 40 regular hours. He had $22.01 deducted this week for health insurance.

NAME		S.S. #		PAY RATE
FIT	FICA	STATE	OTHER	TOTAL DED.
REG. PAY	OVERTIME PAY	GROSS PAY		NET PAY

FIGURE 12-1

TOTAL LOOK BEAUTY SALON	CHECK No. **1266**
1362 SUTTON DRIVE EAST	3523–411
BRANDON, IL 57233	3755

Date _____

PAY TO THE
ORDER OF _____ $ [   ]

_____ DOLLARS

FOSBERG BANK, NA
BRANDON, IL

_____

5724362-770467-1266

FIGURE 12-2

9) George worked 40 regular hours and $5\frac{1}{4}$ hours overtime.

NAME		S.S. #		PAY RATE
FIT	FICA	STATE	OTHER	TOTAL DED.
REG. PAY	OVERTIME PAY	GROSS PAY		NET PAY

FIGURE 12-1

TOTAL LOOK BEAUTY SALON	CHECK No. **1266**
1362 SUTTON DRIVE EAST	3523–411
BRANDON, IL 57233	3755

Date _____

PAY TO THE
ORDER OF _____ $ [   ]

_____ DOLLARS

FOSBERG BANK, NA
BRANDON, IL

_____

5724362-770467-1266

FIGURE 12-2

10) George worked 40 regular hours and 1 hour overtime. He had $22.01 deducted for health insurance and $25.00 for union dues.

NAME		S.S. #		PAY RATE	
FIT	FICA	STATE	OTHER		TOTAL DED.
REG. PAY	OVERTIME PAY	GROSS PAY		NET PAY	

FIGURE 12-1

TOTAL LOOK BEAUTY SALON   CHECK NO. **1266**
1362 SUTTON DRIVE EAST   3523–411
BRANDON, IL 57233   3755

Date _____

PAY TO THE
ORDER OF _____ $ [_____]

_____ DOLLARS

FOSBERG BANK, NA
BRANDON, IL

⑂⑂⑃⑂⑊⑂⑂⑂⑄⑂⑂⑂

_____

FIGURE 12-2

Chapter 13

Personal Finance

Working in the cosmetology profession can provide many benefits. A professional work environment, good wages and benefits, and the ability to provide care for the public are some of the benefits of the career you have chosen. The financial benefits should not be overlooked since they will be important as you provide for yourself and your family.

Managing your money is not difficult, but it does take some self-discipline and some knowledge. There are many opportunities in life to spend money, wisely and unwisely. It is up to you to spend your money wisely, to save enough to provide for emergencies or future goals, and to quickly pay those to whom you owe money.

This chapter will look at checking accounts and savings accounts, which are tools to help you spend and save your money. Then we will look at credit (obtaining credit, using it, and paying the bills that are incurred). Next, we will examine various monthly expenditures that arise when you support yourself (utility bills and groceries), purchasing a car and making payments on it, and renting an apartment. Lastly, we will put all of the expenses together in a monthly budget.

Personal Checking

Having a checking account can be very useful when you have a steady income and monthly expenses. Writing a check is the same as paying cash for an item but it is safer to send through the mail and it eliminates the need to carry large amounts of cash with you.

To open a checking account you must first select a bank. Each bank offers different features in their checking accounts:

- some that make interest;
- some that have service charges (fees that you pay for special services the bank provides);
- some that have an overdraft protection (a certain amount of credit attached to your checking account that prevents a check from bouncing if you do not have enough money in your account);
- some that require a minimum balance (of $200, $500, or more);
- and some that offer extra services.

Once you have selected a bank in which to open your account you must go to that bank and fill out the appropriate application and forms for opening a checking account. You must deposit a certain amount of money (at least the minimum specified by that bank). Then most banks will give you a set of beginner's checks to use until your checks are printed and sent to you.

Once you have opened your checking account, you are authorized to begin writing checks from the amount you have deposited. To write a check you must fill in the following:

- the current date
- the name of the person or organization to whom you are writing the check (called the payee)
- the amount of the check in numbers
- the amount of the check in words
- your signature
- some checks have a memo line where you can make a brief notation to yourself about the purpose of the check

When the check is written it is wise to immediately record that check in the **check register**. This is a record of how much money you currently have in your checking account, according to what you have deposited and what you have spent. To record a check in the check register you must fill in all of the information about the check and subtract the amount of the check from the balance to determine your new checking account balance.

Many banks now have automated teller machines (ATMs) that allow you to draw money out of your account during or after business hours. To use an ATM you need to have an ATM card and a personal identification number (PIN). You insert the ATM card in the ATM and it asks you to enter your PIN. This number should be memorized and guarded carefully since it is what protects your card from being misused by someone else. When you have correctly entered your identification number you can withdraw money. A check does not need to be written but you still must record the transaction in your check register and subtract the amount of the withdrawal from the balance to determine your new checking account balance.

You will also make deposits to your account. To make a deposit you can go to your bank during business hours, use an ATM, or use a night deposit slot (available at most banks). You must fill out a deposit slip, indicating what you plan to deposit and you must sign this deposit slip if you wish to receive any cash back from what you are submitting for deposit. For example, when you go to the bank with your payroll check you may only wish to deposit $100 and you would like the rest back in cash. In this case, your deposit slip must be signed before they will give you the cash back. You should only use the night deposit when you wish to deposit the entire amount since it will not be processed until the next business day. The deposit should also be recorded into your check register and the amount added to the balance to determine your new checking account balance.

To complete a check fill in the date it is being written, the name of the payee, the amount of the check in numbers and also in words (as explained in Chapter 1). Then, sign the check, Figure 13-1.

FIGURE 13-1

To write a deposit slip, fill in the following:

- the date
- your account number
- the amount brought to the bank (usually broken down into coins, currency, and checks)
- the amount you wish to receive in cash
- the amount of the deposit, Figure 13-2.

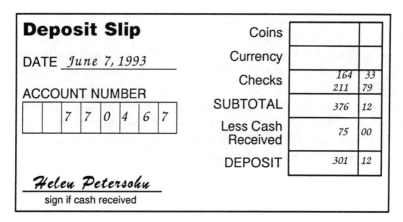

FIGURE 13-2

To fill in the check register for a check or a deposit you must fill in all information requested. A check register usually looks something like Figure 13-3.

Number	Date	Description of Transaction	Payment		x	Deposit		Balance	
								512	79
1274	6/5/93	Phyllis Gordon (cosmetics)	12	57				500	22
	6/7/93	DEPOSIT				301	12	801	34

FIGURE 13-3

1. The number means the number of the check (found in the upper right hand corner)
2. the date is the date the check was written
3. the description of transaction is who the check was written to as well as a description of it's purpose if desired
4. the payment column is for checks or ATM withdrawals or bank fees that come out of your account
5. the deposit column is for deposits or interest earned on the account that goes into your account
6. the balance column records the amount currently in your account

The bank will send you a statement of your account every month. This statement records the deposits, the checks paid out from your account, and the interest earned (or fee charged). They also send you your **cancelled checks**. These are checks that have been written from your account, cashed by the individual the check was written to, and returned to your bank for payment. They are marked cancelled and are proof of the payment you made. They cannot be used again but should be kept for your records along with the statement from the bank.

It is important when you receive your bank statement and cancelled checks that you **reconcile** your checkbook. This is a process of checking to be sure that your records and the bank's records agree. To reconcile your checkbook, you must bring yourself up-to-date on any action that the bank has taken. This would include service charges or interest paid. Write these amounts in your checkbook and either add or subtract the amount to the total (charges = subtract; interest earned = add). Then bring the bank's total up-to-date on any checks you have written or deposits you have made that have not yet come through the bank's computer onto your statement. On a separate paper or on a form the bank might provide (usually on the back of the statement), begin with the bank's total for your account. Add to it any deposits that you have made. Then subtract any checks that you have written that do not appear on the bank statement. This new total should match your new checkbook total. If it does it is said that your checkbook **balanced**. If it does not recheck your work to find your mistake. If you cannot get the two figures to match telephone your bank as soon as possible and ask for help.

Example 1: Write the checks and the deposit slips required and record the following transactions on your check register.

March 15 — Check to Phyllis Gordon for cosmetics $12.57

March 18 — Check to Riegle Electric for February bill $35.22

March 19 — Deposit two checks: $164.33 and $211.79, but receive $75.00 back in cash

HELEN ELAINE PETERSOHN
1362 DANCHEL BOULEVARD
BRANDON, IL 57233

CHECK NO. 1276
3523-411
3788

______________ 19____

PAY TO THE
ORDER OF ____________________ $

____________________________ DOLLARS

FOSBERG BANK, NA
BRANDON, IL

5724362-770467-1276

FIGURE 13-4

HELEN ELAINE PETERSOHN
1362 DANCHEL BOULEVARD
BRANDON, IL 57233

CHECK NO. 1276
3523-411
3788

______________ 19____

PAY TO THE
ORDER OF ____________________ $

____________________________ DOLLARS

FOSBERG BANK, NA
BRANDON, IL

5724362-770467-1276

FIGURE 13-4

Deposit Slip		Coins		
DATE _____		Currency		
		Checks		
ACCOUNT NUMBER		SUBTOTAL		
⬚⬚⬚⬚⬚⬚⬚⬚		Less Cash Received		
		DEPOSIT		
_____ sign if cash received				

FIGURE 13-5

Number	Date	Description of Transaction	Payment	x	Deposit	Balance
						1,531 78

FIGURE 13-6

Problems   Complete the following checks and deposits.

1) Record all checks in problem 1 on this check register.

Number	Date	Description of Transaction	Payment	x	Deposit	Balance
						1,531 78

FIGURE 13-6

Write a check to Barbara Langsley for a haircut ($8.50) on August 12, 19--.

HELEN ELAINE PETERSOHN
1362 DANCHEL BOULEVARD
BRANDON, IL 57233

CHECK No. 1276

3523-411
3788

_____ 19____

PAY TO THE
ORDER OF _____ $ [   ]

_____ DOLLARS

FOSBERG BANK, NA
BRANDON, IL

5724362-770467-1276

_____

FIGURE 13-4

Write a check to Hopewell Gas Company for July bill ($42.38) on August 12, 19--.

HELEN ELAINE PETERSOHN
1362 DANCHEL BOULEVARD
BRANDON, IL 57233

CHECK No. 1276

3523-411
3788

_____ 19____

PAY TO THE
ORDER OF _____ $ [   ]

_____ DOLLARS

FOSBERG BANK, NA
BRANDON, IL

5724362-770467-1276

_____

FIGURE 13-4

Write a check to First Church for an offering ($40.00) on August 14, 19--.

HELEN ELAINE PETERSOHN
1362 DANCHEL BOULEVARD
BRANDON, IL 57233

CHECK No. 1276

3523-411
3788

_____ 19____

PAY TO THE
ORDER OF _____ $ [   ]

_____ DOLLARS

FOSBERG BANK, NA
BRANDON, IL

5724362-770467-1276

_____

FIGURE 13-4

Write a check to Farmer's Electric Company ($21.68) for July electric bill on August 16, 19--.

HELEN ELAINE PETERSOHN
1362 DANCHEL BOULEVARD
BRANDON, IL 57233

CHECK NO. **1276**

3523–411
3788

_____ 19____

PAY TO THE
ORDER OF _____ $ [   ]

_____ DOLLARS

FOSBERG BANK, NA
BRANDON, IL

5724362-770467-1276

FIGURE 13-4

Make a deposit of $4.25 in coins and a check for $350.77 on August 16, 19--.

Deposit Slip

DATE _____

ACCOUNT NUMBER
[| | | | | | | |]

Coins
Currency
Checks
SUBTOTAL
Less Cash Received
DEPOSIT

_____
sign if cash received

FIGURE 13-5

Write a check to Betsy Graham for a decorated cake ($15.50) on August 20,19--.

HELEN ELAINE PETERSOHN
1362 DANCHEL BOULEVARD
BRANDON, IL 57233

CHECK NO. **1276**

3523–411
3788

_____ 19____

PAY TO THE
ORDER OF _____ $ [   ]

_____ DOLLARS

FOSBERG BANK, NA
BRANDON, IL

5724362-770467-1276

FIGURE 13-4

Write a check to Haven Hardware for car parts ($45.22) on August 25, 19--.

HELEN ELAINE PETERSOHN
1362 DANCHEL BOULEVARD
BRANDON, IL 57233

CHECK NO. **1276**

3523–411
3788

_____ 19 ____

PAY TO THE
ORDER OF _____ $ [   ]

_____ DOLLARS

FOSBERG BANK, NA
BRANDON, IL

5724362-770467-1276

FIGURE 13–4

Write a check to Jacob's Jewelry Store ($50.00) for a deposit on a ring on August 27, 19--.

HELEN ELAINE PETERSOHN
1362 DANCHEL BOULEVARD
BRANDON, IL 57233

CHECK NO. **1276**

3523–411
3788

_____ 19 ____

PAY TO THE
ORDER OF _____ $ [   ]

_____ DOLLARS

FOSBERG BANK, NA
BRANDON, IL

5724362-770467-1276

FIGURE 13–4

2) Record all checks in problem 2 on this check register.

Number	Date	Description of Transaction	Payment	x	Deposit	Balance
						1,531 78

FIGURE 13–6

Write a check to Parson's Grocery for a groceries ($56.70) on April 13, 19--.

HELEN ELAINE PETERSOHN
1362 DANCHEL BOULEVARD
BRANDON, IL 57233

CHECK NO. **1276**

3523–411
3788

_____ 19____

PAY TO THE
ORDER OF _____ | $ [   ]

_____ DOLLARS

FOSBERG BANK, NA
BRANDON, IL

5724362-770467-1276

_____

FIGURE 13-4

Write a check to Brighton Land Company for July rent ($240.00) on April 14, 19--.

HELEN ELAINE PETERSOHN
1362 DANCHEL BOULEVARD
BRANDON, IL 57233

CHECK NO. **1276**

3523–411
3788

_____ 19____

PAY TO THE
ORDER OF _____ | $ [   ]

_____ DOLLARS

FOSBERG BANK, NA
BRANDON, IL

5724362-770467-1276

_____

FIGURE 13-4

Write a check to Red Cross for a donation ($30.00) on April 15, 19--.

HELEN ELAINE PETERSOHN
1362 DANCHEL BOULEVARD
BRANDON, IL 57233

CHECK NO. **1276**

3523–411
3788

_____ 19____

PAY TO THE
ORDER OF _____ | $ [   ]

_____ DOLLARS

FOSBERG BANK, NA
BRANDON, IL

5724362-770467-1276

_____

FIGURE 13-4

Write a check to Blanchard Electric Company ($27.83) for March electric bill on April 20, 19--.

HELEN ELAINE PETERSOHN CHECK NO. **1276**
1362 DANCHEL BOULEVARD $\frac{3523-411}{3788}$
BRANDON, IL 57233

_____ 19____

PAY TO THE
ORDER OF _____ | $ [   ]

_____ DOLLARS

FOSBERG BANK, NA
BRANDON, IL

5724362-770467-1276 _____

FIGURE 13-4

Make a deposit of $100.00 in currency and 2 checks: $35.00 and $190.35 on April 21, 19--.

Deposit Slip

DATE _____

ACCOUNT NUMBER
[| | | | | | |]

Coins	
Currency	
Checks	
SUBTOTAL	
Less Cash Received	
DEPOSIT	

_____
sign if cash received

FIGURE 13-5

Write a check to Karen Hanover for a babysitting ($5.50) on April 20,19--.

HELEN ELAINE PETERSOHN CHECK NO. **1276**
1362 DANCHEL BOULEVARD $\frac{3523-411}{3788}$
BRANDON, IL 57233

_____ 19____

PAY TO THE
ORDER OF _____ | $ [   ]

_____ DOLLARS

FOSBERG BANK, NA
BRANDON, IL

5724362-770467-1276 _____

FIGURE 13-4

Write a check to Gross Electric for new lamps ($48.26) on April 25, 19--.

```
┌──────────────────────────────────────────────────────────┐
│  HELEN ELAINE PETERSOHN                CHECK NO. 1276      │
│  1362 DANCHEL BOULEVARD                    3523-411        │
│  BRANDON, IL 57233                           3788          │
│                                  _____ 19____     │
│  PAY TO THE                                                │
│  ORDER OF _____ | $ [_____]      │
│                                                            │
│  _____ DOLLARS        │
│                                                            │
│   FOSBERG BANK, NA                                         │
│      BRANDON, IL                                           │
│   5724362-770467-1276        _____   │
└──────────────────────────────────────────────────────────┘
```

FIGURE 13-4

Write a check to Gonago City Bank ($250.00) for April car payment on April 25, 19--.

```
┌──────────────────────────────────────────────────────────┐
│  HELEN ELAINE PETERSOHN                CHECK NO. 1276      │
│  1362 DANCHEL BOULEVARD                    3523-411        │
│  BRANDON, IL 57233                           3788          │
│                                  _____ 19____     │
│  PAY TO THE                                                │
│  ORDER OF _____ | $ [_____]      │
│                                                            │
│  _____ DOLLARS        │
│                                                            │
│   FOSBERG BANK, NA                                         │
│      BRANDON, IL                                           │
│   5724362-770467-1276        _____   │
└──────────────────────────────────────────────────────────┘
```

FIGURE 13-4

Personal Savings

Having a savings account can be a very wise way to save money when you have a steady income. A savings account usually requires that you keep a minimum balance in the account and interest is earned on that money and any additional that is deposited. The advantage to a savings account over other types of saving—certificates of deposit, U.S. savings bonds, mutual funds, Christmas club accounts, etc.—is that your money is readily available to you. There is no penalty for withdrawal of funds nor are there any requirements on when deposits can be made.

To open a savings account you must first select a bank. Banks vary in the amount of interest they will pay on various savings accounts—usually depending on how much money you are planning to keep in the account (what your minimum balance will be). Once you have selected a bank in which to open your account, you must go to that bank and fill out the appropriate application and forms for opening a savings account. You must deposit a certain amount of money (at least the minimum specified by that bank). You will receive a passbook (similar to a check register) when the account has been opened. This is a book in which you will record all transactions (deposits, withdrawals, and interest earned) that happen with your account.

You can make deposits or withdrawals whenever you wish in your savings account. A deposit is completed like a checking account deposit. A withdrawal of money can be made by filling out a withdrawal form at the bank. The withdrawal form requires the following information:

- date
- account number
- amount in numbers and in words
- your signature

Withdrawal Slip

DATE _____

ACCOUNT NUMBER

AMOUNT

_____ DOLLARS

FIGURE 13-7

Once your account has been opened, you will receive statements from the bank every month, quarter (three months), or other time period agreed upon when you open your account. This statement is similar to a checking account statement. You will need to record the interest you have received in the passbook. Then you should check to see if the bank balance agrees with your own record in the passbook.

Problems Complete the following deposit slips and withdrawal slips for Gina Evans (Acct. No. 46-16333).

1) Deposit $.75 in coins, $25.00 in currency, and $153.67 in checks. No cash received.

Deposit Slip

DATE _____

ACCOUNT NUMBER

	Coins		
	Currency		
	Checks		
	SUBTOTAL		
	Less Cash Received		
	DEPOSIT		

_____
sign if cash received

FIGURE 13-5

2) Withdraw $160.00.

Withdrawal Slip

DATE _____

ACCOUNT NUMBER   AMOUNT

_____ DOLLARS

FIGURE 13-7

3) Deposit 2 checks: $165.99 and $274.83. Receive $45.00 back in cash.

Deposit Slip

DATE _____

ACCOUNT NUMBER

sign if cash received

Coins		
Currency		
Checks		
SUBTOTAL		
Less Cash Received		
DEPOSIT		

FIGURE 13-5

4) Make a deposit of $100.00 in currency, $2.78 in coins, and two checks: $178.55 and $273.71.

Deposit Slip

DATE _____

ACCOUNT NUMBER

sign if cash received

Coins		
Currency		
Checks		
SUBTOTAL		
Less Cash Received		
DEPOSIT		

FIGURE 13-5

5)   Withdraw $271.88.

Withdrawal Slip

DATE _____

ACCOUNT NUMBER

AMOUNT

_____ DOLLARS

FIGURE 13-7

6)   Deposit three checks: $512.22, $173.27, and $25.00. Receive $40.75 back in cash.

Deposit Slip

DATE _____

ACCOUNT NUMBER

	Coins		
	Currency		
	Checks		
	SUBTOTAL		
	Less Cash Received		
	DEPOSIT		

_____
sign if cash received

FIGURE 13-5

7)   Withdraw $176.00.

Withdrawal Slip

DATE _____

ACCOUNT NUMBER

AMOUNT

_____ DOLLARS

FIGURE 13-7

8)   Withdraw $1,747.79.

Withdrawal Slip

DATE _____

ACCOUNT NUMBER

AMOUNT

_____ DOLLARS

FIGURE 13-7

9)   Deposit two checks: $572.44 and $1,376.73 and receive $160.00 back in cash.

Deposit Slip

DATE _____

ACCOUNT NUMBER

Coins

Currency

Checks

SUBTOTAL

Less Cash Received

DEPOSIT

sign if cash received

FIGURE 13-5

10)   Deposit 2 rolls of quarters (worth $10 each), 3 rolls of nickels (worth $2 each), loose coins of $1.57, currency of $675, and a check for $383.76.

Deposit Slip

DATE _____

ACCOUNT NUMBER

Coins

Currency

Checks

SUBTOTAL

Less Cash Received

DEPOSIT

sign if cash received

FIGURE 13-5

Credit

Using credit is the same as borrowing money for an item. When you use credit you are required to pay interest on the balance owed if you don't pay the account in full. Credit should be used with great caution because it often gives "false security"—the feeling that you can afford something that you really cannot.

Types of Credit

There are several different types of credit. Borrowing for a car, a personal loan, a house loan, loans for college, and credit cards are all examples. In this section we will focus on the use of credit cards.

There are different types of credit cards: major credit cards, credit cards from a specific store, gasoline cards, telephone credit cards, etc. The major credit cards are the most difficult to obtain since they usually extend the largest amount of credit (the limit that you are allowed to borrow). These cards almost always charge a yearly fee to use the card and charge interest every month on the unpaid balance. Credit cards from a specific store do not normally charge annual fees, but they do charge interest every month. They usually do not extend as much credit. Gasoline cards often do not charge an annual fee and they normally require you to pay the entire balance at the end of the month. When the balance is not paid, they charge interest on the unpaid balance. Telephone credit cards are similar to gasoline credit cards.

Obtaining Credit

Obtaining credit can be difficult for young people who have never had credit before. It can also be difficult to obtain if you have a bad **credit rating**. Your credit rating is a record of how you have handled credit in the past—how promptly your debts have been paid, how reliable you have been, the extent of your debt, etc.

To apply for credit you are required to fill out an application. Credit applications usually ask for the following information:

- name, address, phone number
- name, address, phone number of relative not living with you (for reference)
- occupation, place of employment, and salary
- work history
- banking information (location, type, and amount of money in accounts held)
- credit history
- references

Using Credit

Credit should be used wisely. Using credit is often easier than paying by cash or check but it should not be abused. The benefits of credit include carrying smaller amounts of cash and knowing that your card will be accepted in a different region of the country. When you are traveling a credit card enables you to reserve hotel rooms in advance, make long distance phone calls with ease, and pay for meals, gasoline, and other necessities.

If you use credit it is wise to follow these guidelines:

- do not charge more than you can afford to pay for each month
- pay all credit card bills *in full* the month you receive them
- do not charge items on impulse that you do not need

If you follow these guidelines you will not have a problem with abusing credit. These suggestions are a strict approach to using credit, but they will help you to avoid many of the problems that arise with credit abuse.

Paying the Bills That Are Incurred.   When you charge items on a credit card, you are sent a monthly statement of that account. The statement shows a record of the purchases and the payments made during the previous month. It indicates your new balance and the minimum amount that you are required to pay. It is best to pay the entire balance at the end of each month but you are only required to pay the minimum amount. The rest of the charge amount will be carried forward to the next month and interest will be assessed.

To pay these bills you simply write a check for the amount you have decided to pay. There is usually a part of the bill that they request you to return to them with your payment. Detach that part of the bill, fill out any information requested, and put that and your check in an envelope and send it to the company. Be sure to record your check on your check register.

Problems   Answer the following questions.

1) List three different types of credit: _____

_____

2) What are three guidelines to use credit wisely? _____

_____

3) What is "false security"? _____

_____

Utility Bills

Under the category of utility bills we will look at all monthly expenses for running a home. These include **household expenses** such as heating (gas, oil, electric, etc.), electricity, telephone, cable television, garbage collection, water, and others. We will also include **fixed expenses** such as taxes and home insurance.

If you own your home you are responsible for all of these expenses and your mortgage payment. If you rent your landlord may provide some of these services—heat, garbage pickup, electricity, insurance for the structure, etc. It is wise for renters to look into property insurance for their possessions however, because the landlord's insurance policy usually will not cover personal possessions. Renter's insurance for possessions is fairly inexpensive and can be a wise investment in case of fire, theft, etc.

Most household expenses are paid monthly. Since the amounts can fluctuate greatly from month to month (due to the weather, greater use, etc.), some companies offer a budget plan. A **budget plan** is a method of paying the same amount each month based on the average amount due. For example, if the electric bills for the previous year ran $45, 40, 40, 35, 55, 50, 50, 45, 55, 60, 65, and 60 for the twelve months, an average amount would be found ($50) and that amount would be charged every month for the following year. If in the final month too much or not enough had been paid to cover the actual costs, an adjustment would be made.

The fixed expenses are usually paid once or twice a year. Since these are usually large amounts, it is wise to save each month for the expense so that when the bill comes, you will have the money to pay it. For example, if the yearly insurance cost is $372, each month's portion is $31 ($372 ÷ 12 = $31). You can save $31 each month and when the bill comes at the end of the 12 months, you will have enough money saved to pay it.

To know how much to set aside to pay fixed expenses:

1. determine how many months the expense covers
   (annual = 12 months, twice a year = 6 months, etc.)

2. divide the amount of the bill by the number of months

Notice in this sample utility bill (Figure 13–8) the following features:

* previous balance
* payment from the previous month
* current balance
* due date
* amount due

Northern Illinois Gas

Date prepared: August 12, 1991

Gas used at: 153 Hope Drive
Your Acct. No: 163167428383

Account Summary

Your meter read 878.7 on Aug. 1
Your meter read 875.3 on July 1
Your usage was 3.4 thousand cubic feet.
Next meter reading will be about
September 1

PREVIOUS BALANCE $13.35
PAYMENT 13.35
CURRENT BILL 17.47
CURRENT BALANCE 17.47

PLEASE PAY: $17.47
BY: Aug. 15, 1991

Monthly Service Charge $ 2.17
3.4 MCF at $4.5 15.30
$17.47

FIGURE 13–8

Problems Read the following utility bills and write a check to the company for the appropriate amount. Date your checks according to the date the bill is due.

1)

Northern Illinois Gas

Date prepared: August 12, 1991

Gas used at: 153 Hope Drive
Your Acct. No: 163167428383

Account Summary

Your meter read 878.7 on Aug. 1
Your meter read 875.3 on July 1
Your usage was 3.4 thousand cubic feet.
Next meter reading will be about
September 1

PREVIOUS BALANCE $13.35
PAYMENT 13.35
CURRENT BILL 17.47
CURRENT BALANCE 17.47

PLEASE PAY: $17.47
BY: Aug. 15, 1991

Monthly Service Charge $ 2.17
3.4 MCF at $4.5 15.30
$17.47

FIGURE 13–9

HELEN ELAINE PETERSOHN
1362 DANCHEL BOULEVARD
BRANDON, IL 57233

CHECK NO. **1276**

3523–411
3788

_____ 19 ____

PAY TO THE
ORDER OF _____ | $ [   ]

_____ DOLLARS

FOSBERG BANK, NA
BRANDON, IL

5724362-770467-1276

FIGURE 13–4

2)

Allied Telephone Company   Pg. 1
March 1, 1991

Business Office: 267-7113   Svc. for: 267-4513

Last Month's Charges		$28.27
Payment	2/6/91	28.27
Adjustments		–0–
Amount Due Previous Bill		.00
TOTAL CURRENT CHARGES		32.78
TOTAL AMOUNT DUE		**$32.78**

DUE BY: 3/10/91

Local Service—Feb. 1 to March 1	27.55
Other Service—Feb. 1 to March 1	3.12
Taxes	2.11
	$32.78

FIGURE 13–10

HELEN ELAINE PETERSOHN
1362 DANCHEL BOULEVARD
BRANDON, IL 57233

CHECK NO. **1276**

3523–411
3788

_____ 19 ____

PAY TO THE
ORDER OF _____ | $ [   ]

_____ DOLLARS

FOSBERG BANK, NA
BRANDON, IL

5724362-770467-1276

FIGURE 13–4

3)

DATE		DESCRIPTION	AMOUNT	BALANCE

ACCOUNT NUMBER: 274-7382-22   **SUBSCRIBER NAME:** Jennifer Myer
DUE DATE: March 9, 1991

DATE		DESCRIPTION	AMOUNT	BALANCE
From	To			
3/1		Previous balance	17.95	
3/1	3/31	Cable television SVC	17.95	
2/7		Prompt payment	17.95	
		AMOUNT DUE		17.95

Make payment to: **ANDERSON CABLE**
1743 VISTA BLVD.
BRANDON, IL 57233

FIGURE 13-11

HELEN ELAINE PETERSOHN   CHECK No. **1276**
1362 DANCHEL BOULEVARD   3523-411
BRANDON, IL 57233   3788

_____19____

PAY TO THE
ORDER OF _____| $ [   ]

_____ DOLLARS

FOSBERG BANK, NA
BRANDON, IL   _____

5724362-770467-1276

FIGURE 13-4

4)

AUSTIN ENTERPRISES   NO. 1372-66
173 RANDALL COURT
BRANDON, IL 57233

For rent at residence   March rent: $370.00
    1674 Raymond Drive West   Due by: 3/15/91
    Brandon, IL 57233

FIGURE 13-12

HELEN ELAINE PETERSOHN   CHECK No. **1276**
1362 DANCHEL BOULEVARD   3523-411
BRANDON, IL 57233   3788

_____19____

PAY TO THE
ORDER OF _____| $ [   ]

_____ DOLLARS

FOSBERG BANK, NA
BRANDON, IL   _____

5724362-770467-1276

FIGURE 13-4

5)

MIDWEST POWER COMPANY
178 Molair Drive
Brandon, IL 57233

SVC. NAME: Jennifer Myers   ACCT. NO. 472747289
1674 Raymond Dr. West.
Brandon, IL 57233

FUEL RATE PER KWH: 1.881690

SERVICE PERIOD		METER READINGS		KWH USED
From	To	Previous	Present	THIS MONTH
2/5	3/5	52687	53204	517

DESCRIPTION	AMOUNT
Balance as of Last Billing Date	36.26
Payment 2/10 Thank You	36.26
Previous Balance	.00
517 KWH Used This Period	38.17
TOTAL	38.17

$1.27 Average Cost a Day
Last Pay. Date—March 10
Pay This Amount $38.17

FIGURE 13–13

HELEN ELAINE PETERSOHN   CHECK No. **1276**
1362 DANCHEL BOULEVARD   3523–411
BRANDON, IL 57233   3788

_____ 19____

PAY TO THE
ORDER OF _____ $ [   ]

_____ DOLLARS

FOSBERG BANK, NA
BRANDON, IL   _____

⑆724362⑈770467⑈1276

FIGURE 13–4

Purchasing a Car

When purchasing a car you have two choices. You can buy a new car or a used one. **New cars** are ones that have had no other owner besides the dealer, whether they are the current year's model or a year old. **Used cars** are ones that have had at least one previous owner. You may buy a used car from that previous owner or from a used car dealer.

Cars are identified by the company that makes them. This identification is called the **make** of the car. For example, a car made by Ford Division of the Ford Motor Company is known as a Ford—this is the make. Then the manufacturer also identifies the car with another name. This is called the **model**. For example, you might go to a Ford dealer and look at several Ford automobiles—the Escort, the Mustang, etc. Then, according to the body type and style the car might be further identified as a **two-door, four-door, hatchback, coupe, sedan, station wagon**, etc.

When you purchase a new car, it is important to shop around to select the make and model that best meets your needs and your budget. Once you've selected the type of car that you are interested in, it is helpful if you can visit more than one dealer to compare prices, service, and selection.

There are different qualities available in used cars. Because of this, you need to be even more aware of what type of car best meets your needs and your budget. You might find that your needs could be met by various makes and models and it will be your goal to get the best car for your money.

When purchasing a used car you need to find out if there is a guarantee on any part or all parts of the vehicle. You will also want to know how many miles the car has been driven (this is found on the **odometer**), the condition of the battery and tires, and general performance of the engine. If you do not have a good understanding of cars it is wise to take a friend or relative along with you when you shop.

On a new car the considerations are different. You will usually be given warranty information. It is also important to understand what guarantee comes with the car and what guarantee features would have to be purchased separately.

In both cases you will want to test drive the vehicle. Use this drive to test all of the accessories (electric locks, windows, radio, etc., especially in a used vehicle). You will also want to consider the appearance and the comfort of the vehicle.

When you have selected the vehicle that you wish to buy you are required to either pay the total amount or make some kind of a down payment. A **down payment** is a partial payment on the vehicle; it can be in the form of cash or a check. Most car dealers will allow you to use a trade-in allowance as part (or all) of your down payment. A **trade-in allowance** is a cash allowance the dealer gives you when you trade your current vehicle in to him in exchange for the newer one. If you make a down payment you will have to get a loan for the remaining amount owed.

A car loan is a type of installment loan. An **installment loan** is a bank loan where you borrow a certain amount and then make monthly payments to repay the principal and the interest. You are usually required to have some collateral on an installment loan, and in most cases the banks use the car as collateral. **Collateral** is property of significant value that the bank could receive if you fail to pay the loan. Since the bank uses the car as collateral you will not have a "clear title" (proof of sole ownership) to the car until you have paid for it entirely.

In most cases, to get a bank loan, you must have some credit established or you must have a co-signer for your loan. A **co-signer** is someone who is willing to bear the responsibility of the loan if you fail to pay it. Being a co-signer should not be taken lightly; it is a large financial and legal responsibility. It is far better for you if you have established credit on your own first and do not need a co-signer for the loan. Credit can be established by applying for (and receiving) credit cards or other loans. To have a good credit rating it is important to pay all credit card bills or loan payments promptly since this information is available to other banks or institutions when you try to receive more credit.

Once the bank agrees to grant you a car loan you will make monthly payments. Out of this payment a certain part goes toward paying off the principal (amount borrowed) and a certain part goes toward paying off the interest (fee charged for the use of the money). At the beginning of a loan the majority of the payment goes toward paying off the interest. The exact amount of the payment that is used to pay off the principal can be figured using a simple process.

To figure the interest, we will use the formula:

$$I = P \times R \times T$$

This stands for Interest = Principal × Rate × Time

To find the amount of the payment going toward interest, we will multiply the principal (amount still due) times the rate (the interest rate, a percent) times the time (1 month—1 out of 12 or 1/12).

This tells us what part of the payment is going toward interest. We can then subtract that amount from the monthly payment to determine how much of the principal has been paid.

Example 1:   The Johnsons recently bought a new car. They obtained a loan for $11,579 at 15% interest. Their monthly payment is $195. How much of the first payment will be put on the interest?

1.   Find the amount going toward interest. $I = P \times R \times T$

$$I = \$11,579 \times 15\% \times \tfrac{1}{12}$$

    change to   multiply by
    decimal   1, divide by
                   twelve

$$= 11,579 \times .15 \times 1 \div 12$$

$$= \$144.7375 \text{ rounds to } \$144.74$$

2.   Find the amount left from the payment to go toward principal.

Principal = Monthly pmt. − interest
            = $195.00 − 144.74
Principal = $ 50.26

3. $50.26 will be put on the principal. We could also find the new balance. We owed $11,579 and have paid $50.26. Our new balance is: $11,579 − 50.26 = $11,528.74.

Problems   Answer the following questions about car loans.

1)   Carolyn Wagner has a loan on her new mini-van. She currently owes $9,572.78. Her monthly payment is $215.75 and her loan has an interest rate of $17\tfrac{1}{4}\%$. What is the new balance on her loan after her next payment?   _____

2)   Kirk Von Kemp recently bought a used two-door sedan. He obtained a loan for $6,000 at 18.5%. His monthly payment is $255.59. What is the amount of the first payment that will go toward interest? What is the amount of the first payment that will go toward principal? How much does he owe on the loan after the first payment?   _____

3)   Delores Hafner pays $215.90 a month for her car payment. She owes $7,500 on the car at an interest rate of $15\tfrac{1}{4}\%$. What is the new balance on her loan after her next payment?   _____

4)   Barb Greensley just bought a Pontorolla Sedan for $15,527.70. She paid $3,000 down and borrowed the remaining amount from the Land Bank of Wilsonville at 16%. She makes monthly payments of $264. What is the amount of the first payment that will go toward interest? What is the amount that will go toward principal? How much does she owe on the loan after the first payment?   _____

5) Alexandria Higgins just bought a sports car for $18,895.95. She used her old car as a down payment (they gave her $4000 credit for it). She borrowed the remaining amount from her bank at 15.5%. She makes monthly payments of $217.78. What does she owe on the loan after the first payment? _____

6) Ray Grove still owes $3648.88 on his Pridemont station wagon. He makes $155.18 car payments and has borrowed the money at 11.5%. How much of his next payment will go toward interest? How much will go toward principal? What will his new balance be? _____

7) August Summerfield wants to pay off the loan on her Jasper mini-van next month. This month she makes a $248.00 car payment. She owes $1579.12 and her loan is at 12% interest. How much will she have to pay next month to pay the entire balance of the loan? _____

8) Tracy Reese needs to make a 15% down payment on the new car she has selected. If it costs $16,840, what will the required down payment be? _____

9) Natasha Vickers picks out a used car that she wishes to buy. It costs $6784.95 and she must pay 25% down. She will borrow the rest from Highlandville Savings and Loan. What will the required down payment be? How much will she borrow from the bank? _____

10) Cathy Crossly wants to buy a truck that costs $15,648.90. She will pay 20% down and borrow the rest from her credit union. Her monthly payments will be $227.99 at $12\frac{1}{4}$% interest. How much of her first payment will go toward interest? How much will go toward principal? What will her new balance be? _____

Housing

There are several choices available in the housing market. When you wish to live out on your own, you can choose between renting or buying. Places available for rent include apartments, townhouses, efficiencies (1 or 2 room apartments), mobile homes, and houses. Places available for purchase include condominiums, mobile homes, and houses. There are a variety of other options available in certain areas with the agreement of the owner or landlord. You can decide to live alone or share the expenses with another individual.

When you consider housing it is important to understand what features are included in your monthly payment. For example, some rental agreements include payment of your utilities. You could expect this to have a higher monthly payment than if you are required to pay for your own utility bills. Some agreements include certain features — perhaps water bill or garbage collection — and not others. Some agreements do not cover any extra features. It is also important to find out how much commitment is involved in the agreement. For example, when renting you may be asked to sign a 1-year lease. This obligates you to pay rent for one year. Or in a purchasing situation you obviously will be bound to your agreement until you can sell to someone else.

There are extra expenses that people often overlook when selecting housing. Do you have to pay a **deposit** (a one-time payment that covers any damage you might do which is refunded when you leave the place in good condition)? Do you have to make a down payment if buying? Is there a **monthly maintenance fee** (a fee collected in some condominium or mobile home situations that pays for grounds upkeep, security, outdoor lighting, etc.)? Is the place furnished or unfurnished? Are drapes and/or carpeting provided? What about insurance, taxes, etc? Be wise in your selection of housing and be sure that you can afford it.

To choose housing you must first decide whether you will rent or buy. Use affordability as a factor, as well as how long you plan to be in the area, how well you know the area, etc. Next, determine how much you can afford to spend on housing (this will be covered in the Monthly Budget section). Decide what area of town you want to be in or whether you would prefer a more rural area. Then begin looking in the classified ads in your local newspaper. Circle options that you would like to consider further and call the realtor or landlord. Ask questions about each place, it's features, extra costs involved, the commitment, etc. Make arrangements to see the places that interest you and then make your decision.

Monthly Budget

The most successful way of handling your money is to use a budget. A **budget** is simply a plan for spending and saving your money. It is not a set of restrictions that you have no control over, but a guideline to help you get the most out of your money.

There are several ways to set up a budget. We will be looking at the percent method, which allocates certain percents of your income for housing, transportation (car payment, insurance, taxes, repairs, etc.), clothing, etc. This helps you to have a balanced spending plan. It can be adjusted to meet your own specific needs. For example perhaps nice housing is really important to you. You may adjust the percent allotted for housing to a higher rate, and then spend less in some other less-important area.

The percents recommended are as follows:

Housing	32%	Entertainment/Recreation	7%
Food	15%	Clothing	5%
Car	15%	Savings	5%
Insurance	5%	Miscellaneous	6%
Debt	5%		

These percents add up to 95%. The remaining 5% may be allotted to a category where there is greater need or to an additional category not considered here. To be successful financially your budget should never exceed 100% of your net spendable income. Use a four-week month whenever weekly income is given. In months with five paydays, the extra check can be used for vacations, Christmas, or other special projects.

To determine how much you can afford in each of these areas, multiply your monthly net spendable income by the appropriate percent. Let's look at a sample budget.

Example 1:   Carole Havner earns $225/weekly (net pay). Determine how much she can afford to spend in each of the above budget categories.

1.   Find her monthly net income ($225 x 4 = $900)

2. Multiply $900 by each percent.

Housing	32% × 900 = $288	Entertainment	7% × 900 =	$ 63
Food	15% × 900 = 135	Clothing	5% × 900 =	45
Car	15% × 900 = 135	Savings	5% × 900 =	45
Insurance	5% × 900 = 45	Miscellaneous	6% × 900 =	54
Debt	5% × 900 = 45	Left-over	5% × 900 =	45

Problems   Determine how much each individual can afford to spend in each of the budget categories.

1) Alicia Grace earns $15,770/yearly net pay.

   a. What is her monthly net pay?   _____

   b. What is her budget amount in:

Housing	_____	Entertainment/Recreation	_____
Food	_____	Clothing	_____
Car	_____	Savings	_____
Insurance	_____	Miscellaneous	_____
Debt	_____	Left-over	_____

2) George DeNisco earns $1662/monthly net pay.

   a. What is his monthly net pay?   _____

   b. What is his budget amount in:

Housing	_____	Entertainment/Recreation	_____
Food	_____	Clothing	_____
Car	_____	Savings	_____
Insurance	_____	Miscellaneous	_____
Debt	_____	Left-over	_____

3) Charlotte Morgan earns $590/weekly net pay.

   a. What is her monthly net pay?   _____

   b. What is her budget amount in:

Housing	_____	Entertainment/Recreation	_____
Food	_____	Clothing	_____
Car	_____	Savings	_____
Insurance	_____	Miscellaneous	_____
Debt	_____	Left-over	_____

4) Harold Bonfilliet earns $27,675/yearly gross pay. Twenty-seven percent of his check is taken out in taxes and other deductions. (Hint: Find his yearly **net** pay first.)

a. What is his monthly net pay?   _____

b. What is his budget amount in:

Housing	_____	Entertainment/Recreation	_____
Food	_____	Clothing	_____
Car	_____	Savings	_____
Insurance	_____	Miscellaneous	_____
Debt	_____	Left-over	_____

5) Austin Long earns $5178/monthly net pay.

a. What is his monthly net pay?   _____

b. What is his budget amount in:

Housing	_____	Entertainment/Recreation	_____
Food	_____	Clothing	_____
Car	_____	Savings	_____
Insurance	_____	Miscellaneous	_____
Debt	_____	Left-over	_____

6) Justine Graham-McGuire earns $37,881/yearly net pay.

a. What is her monthly net pay?   _____

b. What is her budget amount in:

Housing	_____	Entertainment/Recreation	_____
Food	_____	Clothing	_____
Car	_____	Savings	_____
Insurance	_____	Miscellaneous	_____
Debt	_____	Left-over	_____

7) Connie Hawasako earns $23,404/yearly net pay.

a. What is her monthly net pay?   _____

b. What is her budget amount in:

Housing	_____	Entertainment/Recreation	_____
Food	_____	Clothing	_____
Car	_____	Savings	_____
Insurance	_____	Miscellaneous	_____
Debt	_____	Left-over	_____

8) Ray Kildear earns $292.88/weekly net pay.

    a. What is his monthly net pay? _____

    b. What is his budget amount in:

Housing	_____	Entertainment/Recreation	_____
Food	_____	Clothing	_____
Car	_____	Savings	_____
Insurance	_____	Miscellaneous	_____
Debt	_____	Left-over	_____

9) Paul Chung earns $792/monthly net pay.

    a. What is his monthly net pay? _____

    b. What is his budget amount in:

Housing	_____	Entertainment/Recreation	_____
Food	_____	Clothing	_____
Car	_____	Savings	_____
Insurance	_____	Miscellaneous	_____
Debt	_____	Left-over	_____

10) Carissa Rostenkiak earns $92,902/yearly net pay.

    a. What is her monthly net pay? _____

    b. What is her budget amount in:

Housing	_____	Entertainment/Recreation	_____
Food	_____	Clothing	_____
Car	_____	Savings	_____
Insurance	_____	Miscellaneous	_____
Debt	_____	Left-over	_____

Chapter 14

Commercial Discounts

When you own or manage a shop one of your responsibilities will be purchasing. Everything you use in your shop must be purchased as it is needed. This includes the solutions you use for permanents and tints; the equipment you use for rolling, cutting, and styling hair; manicure items; office supplies such as receipts; magazine subscriptions; and a host of other items used in the operation of your shop. It is also very common for beauty salons to carry products in their shop that are available for the customer to purchase. These often include shampoos, styling gels, hair spray, brushes, cosmetics, and a wide variety of other items. These items are purchased on a regular basis, as well as the products you normally use in operating your salon.

Nearly all of the purchases that you make for your shop are bought from a **wholesaler**. A wholesaler is one who purchases items directly from the manufacturer and distributes them to local salons. It is also possible to purchase some items direct from the **manufacturer**. The manufacturer is the company which creates the products (i.e., Nexxus, Revlon, etc.) Whether you buy from a wholesaler or direct from the manufacturer, you will be able to purchase items at a **wholesale** price. This price is often substantially lower than the **list** price, which is the suggested retail price of the item if it were to be sold without any business discounts.

There are many types of discounts available. The two that we will focus on are **trade** discounts and **cash** discounts. Trade discounts are discounts given to retailers (salons) because they often purchase large quantities. Trade discounts provide a way for the supplier (wholesaler or manufacturer) to charge a lower rate to those who purchase in quantity—such as a salon would do. The discount may vary depending on the size of your purchase. By using discounts suppliers can offer lower prices to one group of people than they would another group without creating ill-will. They simply publish one catalog that carries the list price of the items and then offer the appropriate discount to each customer. Then generally the more you buy the larger your discount will be.

With trade discounts it is also possible to provide special sales for items that are selling poorly or to reward large quantity purchases. At times two or more trade discounts may be offered at the same time. These are called **series discounts**. You may receive 20% off and then an additional 5% off as an incentive.

Cash discounts are still a discount that lowers the cost to the retailer, but its purpose is different. A cash discount is offered to encourage prompt, full payment of your bill. Suppliers often offer a 2% discount if you pay within ten days or some similar discount. This benefits you, the retailer, and the supplier because it helps to ensure that they will receive their full payment. It also saves the time and expense of sending additional bills.

Problems   Answer the following questions in complete sentences.

1) Define a supplier and give three examples. _____

    _____

    _____

2) Define a retailer and give three examples. _____

    _____

    _____

3) What is list price? _____

_____

_____

4) What are the two kinds of discounts and why are they offered? _____

_____

_____

_____

5) List 20 things (not counting the examples given above) that you would need to order for a salon.

_____	_____	_____	_____
_____	_____	_____	_____
_____	_____	_____	_____
_____	_____	_____	_____
_____	_____	_____	_____

To buy merchandise it is common to either consult a sales representative from a local supplier or refer to a catalog and then telephone in your order. If you have personal contact with a sales representative you will usually receive a bill or **invoice** at that time. Otherwise, you will either receive it with the items themselves when they are delivered or later, through the mail. When you receive the invoice it is wise to check the items listed against the actual order you received. Was everything delivered that was ordered? Are the quantities correct? It is also wise to check the prices that are listed to be sure they are correct. If the invoice is correctly written check the multiplication and the totals for accuracy. A couple of helpful formulas to remember:

QUANTITY × PRICE PER ITEM = EXTENDED PRICE (TOTAL)

ALL EXTENDED PRICES ADDED = SUBTOTAL OF INVOICE

It is from this subtotal then, that you will apply all of the available discounts offered. The amount that is left after all discounts have been taken is the **net price**.

If it would be necessary to return any items these can be subtracted from the subtotal before applying any discounts. Also, discounts are not applied on shipping and handling charges, labor, or other non-products costs.

Trade Discounts

To find the net price of an invoice multiply the list price by the trade discount rate. This rate is expressed as a percent and must be changed to a decimal before multiplication can be done. This multiplication will yield the trade discount — the actual dollar amount that is being discounted. To find the net price you will subtract this discount from the list price.

LIST PRICE × TRADE DISCOUNT RATE (as decimal) = TRADE DISCOUNT

LIST PRICE − TRADE DISCOUNT = NET PRICE

Problems   Find the trade discount and the net price on each item or group of items below.

	List Price	Discount Rate	Trade Discount	Net Price
1)	$14.95	20%	2.99	11.96
2)	$122.60	$12\frac{1}{2}$%		
3)	$86.33	8%		
4)	$ 5.29	10%		
5)	$99.50	35%		
6)	$115.00	15%		
7)	$42.88	$7\frac{1}{2}$%		
8)	$10.00	4%		
9)	$37.75	20%		
10)	$82.50	22%		
11)	$175.10	5%		
12)	$79.44	11%		
13)	$259.95	$10\frac{1}{2}$%		
14)	$60.25	9%		
15)	$100.00	15%		
16)	$34.72	20%		
17)	$253.10	$15\frac{1}{4}$%		
18)	$30.50	6%		
19)	$374.83	25%		
20)	$92.46	15%		

Total the following invoices then take the appropriate trade discount from the subtotal.

	Qty	Item	List Price	Extension
21)	16	shampoo capes	4.99	
	3	cases perm solution	24.95	
	5	boxes cotton	7.88	
	25	Craylon Shampoo 16 oz.	3.99	
	25	Craylon Gel 4.5 oz.	2.99	
			SUBTOTAL	
			25% TRADE DISCOUNT	
			NET TOTAL	

	Qty	Item	List Price	Extension
22)	25	pr. St. Jay sweatpants	18.99	_____
	40	St. Jay sweatshirts	18.99	_____
	15	St. Jay sunglasses	15.25	_____
	80	St. Jay Shampoo 22 oz.	4.95	_____
	50	St. Jay Hairspray 10 oz.	4.95	_____
			SUBTOTAL	_____
			25% TRADE DISCOUNT	_____
			NET TOTAL	_____

Complement Discounts

Another method of finding trade discounts is called the **complement** method. Consider that the list price represents 100% of the value of the item being purchased. If you are given a 20% discount, how much of the value remains for you to pay? (100% – 20% = _____) You must pay 80% of the list price as your net price.

$$\text{LIST PRICE} \times \text{COMPLEMENT RATE (as decimal)} = \text{NET PRICE}$$

This saves a step in the process, especially if the 100% – discount rate can be done mentally.

Problems   In problems 1–10 find the complement.

1)	45%	_____	6)	10%	_____
2)	25%	_____	7)	18%	_____
3)	50%	_____	8)	5%	_____
4)	$22\frac{1}{2}\%$	_____	9)	35%	_____
5)	20%	_____	10)	11%	_____

In problems 11–30 find the net price using the complement method.

	List Price	Discount Rate	Complement	Net Price
11)	$14.95	20%	.80	11.96
12)	$122.60	$12\frac{1}{2}\%$	_____	_____
13)	$86.33	8%	_____	_____
14)	$ 5.29	10%	_____	_____
15)	$99.50	35%	_____	_____
16)	$115.00	15%	_____	_____
17)	$42.88	$7\frac{1}{2}\%$	_____	_____
18)	$10.00	4%	_____	_____

19)	$37.75	20%	_____	_____
20)	$82.50	22%	_____	_____
21)	$175.10	5%	_____	_____
22)	$79.44	11%	_____	_____
23)	$259.95	$10\frac{1}{2}\%$	_____	_____
24)	$60.25	9%	_____	_____
25)	$100.00	15%	_____	_____
26)	$34.72	20%	_____	_____
27)	$253.10	$15\frac{1}{4}\%$	_____	_____
28)	$30.50	6%	_____	_____
29)	$374.83	25%	_____	_____
30)	$92.46	15%	_____	_____

Series Discounts

Series discounts, as mentioned previously, provide a way to give additional discounts beyond the standard trade discount. They might be offered on items that are selling poorly, items that are new (as an advertising promotion), or as a reward for buying larger quantities. Series discounts look like this: 20%, 10%, 2% or 10%, 5%.

To compute the discounts and the net price, the process is the same as trade discounts but it requires more steps.

Example 1: Cuts-n-Curls purchased products with a list price of $59.95. A series discount of 10%, 5%, and 2% was given. What was the net price?

Step 1: Multiply list price by the first discount rate.

$59.95 × .10 = $5.96

Step 2: Subtract this from the list price.

$59.95 − $5.96 = $53.99 list price after 1st discount

Step 3: Multiply list price after 1st discount by the 2nd discount rate.

$53.99 × .05 = $2.70

Step 4: Subtract this from the list price after 1st discount.

$53.99 − $2.70 = $51.29 list price after 2nd discount.

Step 5: Multiply list price after 2nd discount by the 3rd discount rate.

$51.29 × .02 = $1.03

Step 6: Subtract this from the list price after 2nd discount.

$51.29 − $1.03 = $50.26 NET PRICE

Continue this until all discounts have been applied.

Example 2:   Regents Salons purchased products for their national salon chain with a value of $2,569.95. A series discount of 25%, 10%, and 5% was given. What was the net price?

1st discount: $2569.95 × .25 = $642.49
$2569.95 − $642.49 = $1927.46

2nd discount: $1927.46 × .10 = $192.75
$1927.46 − $192.75 = $1734.71

3rd discount: $1734.71 × .05 = $86.74
$1734.71 − $86.74 = $1647.97

Problems   Find the following series discounts and the final net price for the problems below:

List price	Series discounts	Discounts	Net Price
1) $ 529.50	25% 5%	1st_____	_____
		2nd_____	_____
2) $ 1,252.99	25% 10% 2%	1st_____	_____
		2nd_____	_____
		3rd_____	_____
3) $ 67.88	10% 5%	1st_____	_____
		2nd_____	_____
4) $ 427.95	10% 5% 2%	1st_____	_____
		2nd_____	_____
		3rd_____	_____
5) $ 859.15	10% 7% 5%	1st_____	_____
		2nd_____	_____
		3rd_____	_____
6) $ 162.73	5% 2%	1st_____	_____
		2nd_____	_____
7) $ 923.71	15% 10% 5%	1st_____	_____
		2nd_____	_____
		3rd_____	_____
8) $ 1,380.37	25% 10% 2%	1st_____	_____
		2nd_____	_____
		3rd_____	_____
9) $ 1,380.37	20% 10% 5%	1st_____	_____
		2nd_____	_____
		3rd_____	_____

10) $ 284.28   10% 2%   1st_____   _____

                                                2nd_____   _____

11) $ 167.83   8% 5% 2%   1st_____   _____

                                                2nd_____   _____

                                                3rd_____   _____

12) $ 815.22   20% 10% 5%   1st_____   _____

                                                2nd_____   _____

                                                3rd_____   _____

13) $ 1,773.35   10% 2%   1st_____   _____

                                                2nd_____   _____

14) $ 932.64   15% 10% 2%   1st_____   _____

                                                2nd_____   _____

                                                3rd_____   _____

15) $ 227.38   20% 10% 7%   1st_____   _____

                                                2nd_____   _____

                                                3rd_____   _____

Single Equivalent Discounts

The process of finding series discounts can be simplified greatly when you apply the complement method. In reviewing a single discount problem we know that finding a 20% discount and subtracting it from the list price (100% of the value) is the same as finding 80% of the item.

   Using this same concept, the **single equivalent discount** method uses the complements of a series of discounts to solve a series discount problem. Let's review Example 1 given in the series discount section.

Example 1:   Cuts-n-Curls purchased products with a list price of $59.95. A series discount of 10%, 5%, and 2% was given. What was the net price?

   Step 1:   Multiply list price by the first discount rate.

               $59.95 × .10 = 6.00

   Step 2:   Subtract this from the list price.

               $59.95 − $6.00 = $53.95 list price after 1st discount

   Step 3:   Multiply list price after 1st discount by the 2nd discount rate.

               $53.99 × .05 = $2.70

   Step 4:   Subtract this from the list price after 1st discount.

               $53.95 − $2.70 = $51.25 list price after 2nd discount

   Step 5:   Multiply list price after 2nd discount by the 3rd discount rate.

               $51.25 × .02 = $1.03

Step 6:   Subtract this from the list price after 2nd discount.

$$\$51.25 - \$1.03 = \$50.22 \ \text{NET PRICE}$$

Instead of six steps which consisted of multiplying then subtracting, multiplying then subtracting, multiplying then subtracting, we can use complements.

Step 1:   The complement of 10% is 90% (.90)
The complement of 5% is 95% (.95)
The complement of 2% is 98% (.98)

Step 2:   We can multiply these complements together to find our **single equivalent discount (SED)**.

$$.90 \times .95 \times .98 = 0.8379 \ \text{This is our SED.}$$

Step 3:   Multiply the list price × SED to determine net price.

$$\$59.95 \times .8379 = \$50.23 \ \text{NET PRICE}$$

The result is one cent different that doing the long method because of variations in rounding the intermediate steps. Either answer is acceptable.

Problems   Find the SED for the following series discounts.

1) 10%, 5%, 3% _____   11) 25%, 20%, 5% _____

2) 15%, 10%, 2% _____   12) 30%, 10%, 2% _____

3) 10%, 10%, 2% _____   13) 35%, 10%, 5% _____

4) 15%, 5% _____   14) 25%, 10% _____

5) 25%, 15%, 5% _____   15) 40%, 10% _____

6) 10%, 2% _____   16) 22.5%, 5% _____

7) 10%, 5% _____   17) 12%, 8% _____

8) 15%, 3% _____   18) 40%, 15% _____

9) 40%, 20%, 2% _____   19) 15%, 5%, 3% _____

10) 20%, 5% _____   20) 20%, 15%, 10%, 5% _____

Complete the following:

	List Price	Discount Series	SED	Net Price
21)	$ 157.95	15%, 10%, 5%	_____	_____
22)	$1,252.57	20%, 10%	_____	_____
23)	$ 672.38	35%, 10%, 5%	_____	_____
24)	$ 163.82	20%, 5%	_____	_____
25)	$3,627.92	35%, 20%, 10%	_____	_____

Cash Discounts

Cash discounts are computed in the same manner as trade discounts but they serve a different purpose. They are an incentive offered by suppliers so that retailers will pay their bills promptly.

The cash discounts that you might receive will depend on how promptly you pay each particular bill. Each invoice is generally coded to show you the discount that is available for prompt payment. This coding can be found on your bill under the heading **terms**. The terms of sale spell out the conditions under which you might qualify for a cash discount. For example the terms of sale might look like this: 2/10, net/30. This means that a 2% discount is being offered if the bill is paid within 10 days (from the date on the invoice) and the net price must be paid within 30 days.

To avoid confusion on dates, some suppliers offer terms that begin at the end of the month in which the bill is being issued (EOM). The terms 2/10, net/30 EOM means 2% discount if paid within 10 days after the end of the month and the net price must be paid within 30 days after the end of the month. For example if the invoice is dated March 28 the counting of days begins April 1. The 2% discount is available through April 10 and the net price must be paid by April 30.

Another way to date the terms involves dating by the ROG (receipt of goods) method. This means that the terms begin upon receipt of the items. The terms 2/10, net/30 ROG means a 2% discount if paid within 10 days after the items are received. The net price must be paid within 30 days after the items are received. For example the invoice is dated June 26 but the items do not arrive until June 29. Ten days later would be July 9 and thirty days later would be July 29. Notice that June 29 is not counted; the counting begins the following day.

Terms can also include various stages of discount. For example, 3/10, 2/20, net/30 means a 3% discount if paid within 10 days, a 2% discount if paid within 20 days and the net price must be paid within 30 days.

Problems   Determine the last day that a discount would be offered on the following terms.

Date of Invoice	Terms	Last day for Discount
1) May 29	2/10, net 30	_____
2) August 14	3/10, net 30 EOM	_____
3) December 29	5/5, net 30	_____
4) January 16	3/10, net 30	_____
5) October 27	2/10, net 30 EOM	_____

Find the cash discount and the amount due for each item listed.

6) Kelsey was paying a bill dated May 29 with the terms 2/10, 3/20, net 30 ROG. The items were received June 6. The net price of the bill was $157.69. What is the amount of discount that Kelsey will receive? What is the cash price?   _____

7) Stephanie was paying a bill dated November 11 with the terms 2/10, net 30 EOM. The items were received November 25 and she paid the bill that day. The price of the bill was $297.37. What is the amount of discount that she will receive? What is the cash price?   _____

8) Janet is ordering items to sell in her shop. Jovia Supply and Cascade Supply both offer the same net price for the items that she wishes to order. Jovia has a cash discount of 2/10, net 30 ROG and Cascade has a cash discount of 3/10, net 30. She is placing the order October 11 but is planning to be out of town until October 24. Delivery is available from either supply store while she is gone, but she is concerned about paying her bill. Which supply store should she choose and why?   _____

9) Hope Harrison is paying a bill dated July 17 with terms of 3/10, 2/20, net/30 EOM. She received the items July 22. She is paying the invoice August 17. If the net price is $517.82, what will her cash discount be? What is the cash price?   _____

10) Jenna is paying an invoice date December 20 with terms of 4/10, 3/20, net/30. She received the items December 23. If the invoice totals $1,672.36 and she pays the bill January 11, what will her cash discount be? What is the cash price?   _____

Chapter 15

Business Finance

Sales Tax

If you sell products in your shop, you often are required to collect state or local sales tax in addition to the price of the products. Some states or localities may not require a sales tax, but most do. These sales taxes are generally a certain percentage of the price of the item. For example, your state may require a 5% sales tax and the city that your shop operates in might require a 1% sales tax. If this is the case, you would charge your customers for the cost of the items purchased plus an additional 6%. These taxes are held in reserve in your bank account and paid out to the appropriate government agency (state or local) on a regular basis.

Example 1:   Claire's Boutique sold $15.95 worth of hair care products to Sharon Wheeler. If the state sales tax rate is $4\frac{1}{2}$% and the local rate is 1%, what is the total sales tax? What is the total amount due by Sharon?

- $4\frac{1}{2}$% = 4.5 %: to decimal = .045 and 1 % = .01

- .045 + .01 = .055 tax rate

- $15.95 × .055 = $.87725 which rounds to $.88 sales tax

- $15.95 + .88 = $16.83 total amount due

Example 2:   Reese's Salon has sold $15,627.93 worth of hair care and cosmetic products this year. If the state tax rate is 5%, what will be the amount of state sales tax that must be forwarded to the state?

$15,627.93 × .05 = $781.3965 rounds to $781.40

Problems   Determine the amount of sales tax and the total purchase price for the following transactions:

	Cost of Items	State Tax Rate	Local Tax Rate	Total Tax	Total Purchase Price
1)	$16.37	$4\frac{1}{4}$%	$\frac{1}{2}$%	_____	_____
2)	$37.99	4%	1%	_____	_____
3)	$6.95	3.5 %		_____	_____
4)	$25.00	$4\frac{3}{4}$%	$\frac{3}{4}$%	_____	_____
5)	$29.50	5%		_____	_____
6)	$82.93		2%	_____	_____
7)	$9.99	$5\frac{1}{2}$%	$\frac{1}{2}$%	_____	_____
8)	$21.88	3%	1%	_____	_____

9) $11.03 $2\frac{1}{2}$% $\frac{1}{4}$%   _____   _____

10) $31.38   4%   _____   _____

11) $1.88   5% $\frac{1}{2}$%   _____   _____

12) $10.04   3% $\frac{1}{4}$%   _____   _____

13) $100.67 $4\frac{3}{4}$% $\frac{1}{2}$%   _____   _____

14) $7.99   2%   _____   _____

15) $9.33 $4\frac{1}{2}$%   _____   _____

Determine the amount of taxes due to the following government agencies at the end of the tax period:

16)   Gretta's House of Beauty assesses 5% state sales tax and $\frac{1}{2}$% city tax. Her sales for the months of October through December were: October $357.88, November $163.99, and December $1,274.92. How much state sales tax must she send in for that three month period? How much local sales tax must she send in for the same time period?   _____

17)   Hudson's assesses $4\frac{1}{4}$% state sales tax. The salon sells clothing, cosmetics, and hair care products. They also sell some packaged foods, which are not subject to sales tax. The sales for January through June were as follows:

Month	Non-food Sales	Food Sales
January	3,539.35	421.63
February	1,734.73	256.72
March	2,372.82	173.82
April	931.63	488.36
May	1,613.71	126.36
June	1,003.36	621.78

What was Hudson's total sales for the first six months of the year? What part of that total is subject to state sales tax? What is the amount of state sales tax to be submitted based on the sales from January through June?   _____

18)   Laura's Clips-n-Curls sells Millani Hair Care products. The manager is required to assess $3\frac{1}{2}$% sales tax on these items which must be turned in on a monthly basis. Determine the amount of sales tax that must be sent in every month for the following sales:

January	$ 137.83	_____	July	$ 183.27	_____
February	361.71	_____	August	93.33	_____
March	216.82	_____	September	163.66	_____
April	361.63	_____	October	261.78	_____
May	215.76	_____	November	478.93	_____
June	127.27	_____	December	642.72	_____

19)   Gals-n-Guys is required to collect 5% sales tax on all purchases. What is the amount of sales tax collected on sales of $521.55 for a three-month period?   _____

20) Miriam's is required to collect 4% sales tax on all purchases. To simplify matters for her customers, however, she has included the sales tax in with the price of each item. How much sales tax should be submitted to the state if her total purchases for a month are listed as $1,631.63? HINT: The total purchases represents 100% of the price of the item plus 4% sales tax—thus 104%. You will need to set up a proportion: 4% is to 104% as the tax is to the total.

OR
$$\frac{.04}{1.04} = \frac{\text{tax}}{1,631.63}$$

Business Loans

When you own or operate your own business it is often necessary to borrow money. This might be needed to buy or to upgrade your equipment. Most often money is borrowed from a bank and regular monthly payments are required to pay back the money borrowed (principal) plus the interest assessed. Occasionally a loan involves one lump-sum payment at the end of the loan.

There are various ways to compute the interest involved in borrowing. One way is **simple** interest. This is used to determine the amount of interest that is due over the entire length of the loan, when there is to be one lump-sum payment. Simple interest can be found using the formula:

$$\text{INTEREST} = \text{PRINCIPAL} \times \text{RATE} \times \text{TIME}$$

where interest is found by multiplying the **principal** times the interest **rate** (as a decimal) and then multiplying by the length of the loan or **time** (expressed as a part of a year).

To express the length of the loan, it is necessary to know for what part of a year or how many total years the loan is being issued.

Example 1: Determine the time for a three month loan. It is 3 months out of 12 possible or $\frac{3}{12}$, which reduces to $\frac{1}{4}$. Thus, you would multiply by .25 ($\frac{1}{4}$ changed to a decimal).

Example 2: Determine the time for a 36-month loan. It is 36 months out of 12 in a year or $\frac{36}{12}$. This reduces to 3, thus you would multiply by 3.

When the loan is issued over a given number of days you need to know how the bank computes interest. **Exact** interest uses an actual 365 day year. **Ordinary** interest rounds the length of the year to 360 days, considered to be 30 days in each month. Once you know which method is used, you can determine the time.

Example 3: Compute ordinary interest for a loan lasting 45 days. The time would be 45 days out of 360 possible, $\frac{45}{360}$. This reduces to $\frac{1}{8}$, which must then be changed to a decimal (0.125).

Example 4: Find the same length of loan involving exact interest. Exact interest involves 365 days, so $\frac{45}{365} = \frac{9}{73}$ which as a decimal rounds to 0.1233.

Problems   Find the time for the following problems. When necessary, round to the 10,000th place.

1) 63 days, ordinary _____   11) 4 months   _____

2) 120 days, ordinary_____   12) 73 days, exact   _____

3) 60 months   _____   13) 192 days, ordinary _____

4) 27 months   _____   14) 146 days, exact   _____

5) 47 days, exact   _____   15) 18 months   _____

6) 365 days, exact   _____   16) 42 months   _____

7) 125 days, ordinary_____   17) 80 days, ordinary   _____

8) 14 months   _____   18) 100 days, exact   _____

9) 2 months   _____   19) 270 days, ordinary _____

10) 60 days, ordinary _____   20) 30 months   _____

Exact and ordinary interest are similar to simple interest in that interest is computed once over the life of the loan using the formula:

$$INTEREST = PRINCIPAL \times RATE \times TIME$$

Once interest is determined by multiplying principal times rate times time, it must be added to the principal to determine the total amount due on the loan.

$$PRINCIPAL + INTEREST = TOTAL\ AMOUNT\ DUE$$

Example 1:   Greg's Barber Shop wants to borrow $5000 to remodel. His loan is payable in 36 months at an interest rate of $10\frac{1}{4}\%$. How much interest will he pay and what will be the total amount due?

$$INTEREST = PRINCIPAL \times RATE \times TIME$$

$$interest = \$5000 \times 10.25\% \times \tfrac{36}{12}$$
$$interest = 5000 \times .1025 \times 3$$
$$interest = \$1537.50$$

$$PRINCIPAL + INTEREST = TOTAL\ AMOUNT\ DUE$$

$$\$5000 + \$1537.50 = total\ amount\ due$$
$$\$6537.50 = total\ amount\ due$$

Example 2:   Janet DeRonda borrowed $1000 for 50 days. The exact interest rate is 12%. What is the interest on the loan? (Do not round until the final answer, then round to the nearest cent)

$$INTEREST = PRINCIPAL \times RATE \times TIME$$
$$interest = 1000 \times .12\% \times \tfrac{50}{365}$$

At this point, instead of dividing 50 by 365 to find time like we have been (which forces us to round), carry out the entire problem with continuous operations. Multiply 1000 by .12. Multiply that product by 50. Then, take that product and divide it by 365. Round the final answer.

$$1000 \times .12 = 120$$
$$120 \times 50 = 6000$$
$$\tfrac{6000}{365} = 16.438 \text{ which rounds to } \$16.44$$

Problems Compute the interest and total amount due for the following ordinary interest problems. Do not round until the final step in finding interest.

	Principal	Rate	Time	Interest	Total Amount Due
1)	$1000	$12\frac{1}{2}\%$	60 days	_____	_____
2)	$5000	$8\frac{1}{4}\%$	45 days	_____	_____
3)	$2550	10%	100 days	_____	_____
4)	$400	$9\frac{1}{2}\%$	80 days	_____	_____
5)	$2050	9%	320 days	_____	_____

Compute the interest and total amount due for the following exact interest problems. Do not round until the final step in finding interest.

	Principal	Rate	Time	Interest	Total Amount Due
6)	$3000	$10\frac{1}{4}\%$	185 days	_____	_____
7)	$2400	$9\frac{1}{2}\%$	108 days	_____	_____
8)	$550	10%	45 days	_____	_____
9)	$1390	7%	165 days	_____	_____
10)	$775	$7\frac{3}{4}\%$	290 days	_____	_____

Compute the interest and total amount due for the following simple interest problems. Do not round until the final step in finding interest.

	Principal	Rate	Time	Interest	Total Amount Due
11)	$2000	10%	14 months	_____	_____
12)	$3500	$8\frac{1}{2}\%$	36 months	_____	_____
13)	$4050	10%	18 months	_____	_____
14)	$500	7%	7 months	_____	_____
15)	$6000	$9\frac{3}{4}\%$	27 months	_____	_____

We have been looking at single payment loans, where interest is computed once over the life of the loan and there is one large payment at the end of the loan. However most business loans are **installment** loans. Installment loans are loans where you make monthly payments each month over the life of the loan. These monthly payments go towards paying interest and principal both. The interest is computed every month (for *one* month of the loan) and it is paid first out of the payment. Whatever is left goes toward paying off the principal.

Example 1: Kathryn LeMar borrowed $1000 at 18% for 12 months. Her monthly payments are $91.68. How much of her first payment goes toward interest and how much goes toward principal? What is her new balance after one month?

1) INTEREST = PRINCIPAL × RATE× TIME
   interest   =   1000   ×   .18 × $\frac{1}{12}$ (on installment loans you are always
   looking at 1 month out of 12 possible)

   interest   = $15.00

2) PAYMENT − INTEREST = AMOUNT PUT ON PRINCIPAL
   $91.68   −   15.00   = $76.58 on principal

3) ORIGINAL PRINCIPAL − AMOUNT PUT ON PRINCIPAL = NEW BALANCE
   $1000   −   76.58   = $923.42

It is possible to carry this out further, determining the second months' activities and the third months' and so on throughout the life of the loan. It is important to remember however, that once a payment has been made your principal decreases. You would use NEW BALANCE × RATE × TIME to determine interest for the next month, instead of the original principal.

Example 2:   Find the second and third months' activity on Kathryn's loan.

1) INTEREST = PRINCIPAL × RATE× TIME   (use new balance)
   interest   =   923.42   ×   .18 × $\frac{1}{12}$ (on installment loans you are always
   looking at 1 month out of 12 possible)

   interest   = $13.85

2) PAYMENT − INTEREST = AMOUNT PUT ON PRINCIPAL
   $91.68   −   13.85   = $77.83 on principal

3) PREVIOUS BALANCE − AMOUNT PUT ON PRINCIPAL = NEW BALANCE
   $923.42   −   77.83   = $845.59

REPEAT FOR THE FOLLOWING MONTH:

1) INTEREST = PRINCIPAL × RATE× TIME   (use new balance)
   interest   =   845.59   ×   .18 × $\frac{1}{12}$ (on installment loans you are always
   looking at 1 month out of 12 possible)

   interest   = $12.68

2) PAYMENT − INTEREST = AMOUNT PUT ON PRINCIPAL
   $91.68   −   12.68   = $79.00 on principal

3) PREVIOUS BALANCE − AMOUNT PUT ON PRINCIPAL = NEW BALANCE
   $845.59   −   79.00   = $766.59

Problems   Solve the following problems, showing your work.

1) Janice borrowed $3000 at 18% for 36 months. Her monthly payments were $108.46. On her first month's payment what amount was applied toward interest and toward principal? What is her new balance at the end of the first month?
   _____

2) Mrs. Gresemyer borrowed $5000 at $15\frac{1}{2}$% for 24 months. Her monthly payments were $243.62. On her first month's payment what amount was applied toward interest and toward principal? What is her new balance at the end of the first month?   _____

3) Trent Fowler borrowed $8000 at $13\frac{1}{2}$% for 30 months. His monthly payments were $315.68. On his first month's payment what amount was applied toward interest and toward principal? What is his new balance at the end of the first month?   _____

4) Find the amount of payment applied toward interest and toward principal and the new balance on Trent's second month.   _____

5) Find the amount of payment applied toward interest and toward principal and the new balance on Trent's third month.   _____

Answer Key

Answer Key

Chapter 1 Problems

Place Values

1) 10th	7) 10,000	13) 10th	19) 10,000	23) 3	27) 7
3) 100th	9) 100th	15) 100s	21) 2	25) 0	29) 8
5) 100s	11) 10,000th	17) 10s			

Comparing Numbers

a. The largest numbers in each set are:

1) 4.786	7) 486	13) 2173	19) 53	23) 2577	27) 7676
3) 6.2	9) 49300	15) 6200	21) 151.1	25) 2.65	29) 8100
5) 700	11) 15	17) 26.3			

b. The number not equal to the others is:

31) 8.100   33) 1002.0   35) .1010

Rounding Numbers

1) 57,000	3) 3,000	5) 2,000	7) 877,000	9) 27,648,000
1) 57,300	3) 3,200	5) 2,200	7) 876,500	9) 27,647,500
1) 57,260	3) 3,180	5) 2,180	7) 876,520	9) 27,647,530
1) 5	3) 52	5) 214	7) 4	9) 5
1) 4.8	3) 51.7	5) 213.6	7) 4.0	9) 5.2
1) 4.78	3) 51.67	5) 213.62	7) 4.01	9) 5.15
1) 4.777	3) 51.673	5) 213.617	7) 4.006	9) 5.152
1) 4.8	3) 2.1	5) 4	7) 2100	9) 21,800
11) 3.755	13) 150	15) 360	17) 9.00	

Reading and Writing Numbers

1) 4 thousand 2 hundred 96 and 81 hundredths
3) 74 and 6 hundred 59 thousandths
5) three
7) 81 thousand 2 hundred 67 and 5 thousand 8 hundred 32 ten-thousandths
9) 27 and 3 ten-thousandths
11) 53 thousand 2 hundred 74 and 83 hundredths
13) 1 and 5 thousandths
15) 45 ten-thousandths
17) 17 thousand 3 hundred 44 and 47 hundredths
19) 1 million 6 hundred 94 thousand 8 hundred 69
21) 37 and 97 hundredths
23) 8 hundred 82 and 22 hundredths
25) 23 and 6 thousand 3 hundred 75 ten-thousandths
27) 28 thousand 5 hundred 87
29) 16 and 33 thousand 6 hundred 85 hundred-thousandths

Chapter 2 Problems

Addition

1) 31	5) 43	9) 54	13) 5179	17) 203	21) 578, 28, 1394, 957
3) 29	7) 88	11) 5159	15) 1689	19) 90373	23) 78, 32

Subtraction

1) 6	5) 68	9) 27	13) 3831	17) 586	21) 211, 9, 399, 432
3) 63	7) 32	11) 675	15) 441	19) 320	23) 28, 16, 0

Multiplication

1) 70	5) 42	9) 192	13) 6,004,532	17) 5,733	21) $38, $18
3) 66	7) 225	11) 16,192	15) 671,328	19) 11,468,000	23) $2,696

Division

1) 6 R 36	5) 6 R 8	9) 28 R 32	13) 51 R 7	17) 92 R 49	21) $272
3) 122 R 4	7) 16 R 44	11) 202	15) 83 R 39	19) 912 R 12	23) 269 hrs; no

Mixed Operations

1) 45	5) $147	9) 336	13) 625	17) $1,001, $2,444, yes
3) $14	7) 662	11) 41	15) $780	

Chapter 3 Problems

Addition

1) 125.403	5) 244.3951	9) 119	13) $276.348	17) $324.65, $320.54,
3) 1.0000	7) 223.242	11) $400.06	15) 3.525%	$885.20, $347.23

Subtraction

1) 26.769	5) 8961.7996	9) 1743.9	13) $.64	17) Green; $47.75
3) 1.016	7) .01	11) $1529.13	15) $14.70	

Multiplication

1) .006007	5) .040405	9) 89.7204	13) $14.96; 6.51; 23.40	17) $1553.64
3) 257.792	7) 8339.1	11) $481.25	15) 42.5; 33.75; 40; 31.5	

Division

1) 1.56	5) 8.04	9) 22.89	13) $13.34
3) 235.5	7) 4.18	11) $.09	15) Brand A $.23; Brand B $.22; Brand B

Mixed Operations

1) 231.28	5) Gladwell $.59; Frampton $.54;	7) 39.2 mi	11) $1981.83; $495.46
3) $.91/hr	Frampton is cheaper by $.05/oz.	9) $9.77	13) $236.59; $39.43

Chapter 4 Problems

Least Common Denominator

1) 35	5) 24	9) 60	13) $\frac{6}{9}$; $\frac{4}{9}$	17) $\frac{12}{18}$; $\frac{15}{18}$ — $\frac{5}{6}$
3) 10	7) 40	11) $\frac{36}{84}$; $\frac{77}{84}$	15) $\frac{48}{60}$; $\frac{35}{60}$	19) $\frac{35}{42}$; $\frac{24}{42}$ — $\frac{5}{6}$

Reducing Fractions

1) $\frac{1}{8}$	5) $\frac{1}{6}$	9) $\frac{2}{3}$	13) $\frac{5}{17}$	17) $\frac{2}{9}$
3) $\frac{1}{4}$	7) $\frac{2}{7}$	11) $\frac{2}{5}$	15) $\frac{3}{4}$	19) $\frac{1}{8}$

Mixed Numbers

1) $\frac{30}{7}$ 9) $\frac{83}{8}$ 17) $\frac{19}{4}$ 23) $4\frac{2}{5}$ 29) 2   35) $9\frac{1}{6}$

3) $\frac{32}{6}$ 11) $\frac{13}{3}$ 19) $\frac{31}{7}$ 25) $8\frac{2}{5}$ 31) $5\frac{1}{3}$ 37) $3\frac{3}{5}$

5) $\frac{13}{4}$ 13) $\frac{23}{6}$ 21) $3\frac{3}{4}$ 27) $2\frac{2}{7}$ 33) $13\frac{1}{3}$ 39) $22\frac{1}{2}$

7) $\frac{20}{3}$ 15) $\frac{25}{9}$

Addition

1) $8\frac{14}{15}$ 5) $3\frac{17}{36}$ 9) $8\frac{17}{40}$ 13) $1\frac{79}{120}$

3) $8\frac{39}{70}$ 7) $1\frac{1}{20}$ 11) $28\frac{3}{4}$; $24\frac{3}{8}$; $33\frac{14}{45}$; $142\frac{1}{5}$; $1357\frac{5}{12}$

Subtraction

1) $\frac{1}{8}$ 5) $\frac{23}{60}$ 9) $\frac{5}{24}$ 13) $3\frac{4}{9}$ 17) 4 c; $3\frac{7}{8}$ c

3) $\frac{11}{70}$ 7) $\frac{1}{5}$ 11) $2\frac{1}{2}$ 15) $2\frac{7}{10}$ 19) $889\frac{3}{4}$

Multiplication

1) $1\frac{7}{18}$ 7) $1\frac{9}{16}$ 13) $26\frac{2}{7}$ 19) 9   25) $\$53\frac{1}{8}$

3) $\frac{21}{40}$ 9) $1\frac{3}{8}$ 15) $16\frac{1}{4}$ 21) $3\frac{15}{16}$; $4\frac{5}{8}$; $3\frac{5}{12}$; $1\frac{25}{32}$; $3\frac{1}{20}$

5) $1\frac{1}{12}$ 11) $3\frac{39}{50}$ 17) $26\frac{19}{20}$ 23) 6; 5; $7\frac{1}{3}$; $9\frac{1}{4}$

Division

1) $2\frac{1}{3}$ 5) $\frac{3}{11}$ 9) 1   13) 4   17) $3500

3) 2   7) $1\frac{31}{33}$ 11) 8   15) 11   19) 120

Mixed Operations

1) 49 oz.   5) $\$53\frac{13}{16}$ or \$53.81   7) $27\frac{5}{8}$ 9) $\frac{3}{5}$

3) $15\frac{1}{2}$; $11\frac{3}{8}$; $\frac{9}{16}$; none

Chapter 5 Problems

Percents to Decimals

1) .55   7) .49   13) .10   19) .00361   25) .45   31) $27\frac{1}{2}$%; .275

3) .65   9) .74   15) .081   21) .71   27) .01   33) .79

5) 1 (or 1.00)   11) 1.255   17) 3.722   23) .05   29) .036   35) .1875

Decimals to Percents

1) 57.8%   7) 11.1%   13) 530%   19) 88%   25) .1%   31) 4.5%

3) 73.14%   9) 60%   15) 722%   21) 6400%   27) .5%   33) .7; 70%

5) 400%   11) .7%   17) 333%   23) .06%   29) 1350%   35) 45%

Decimals to Fractions

1) $4\frac{14}{25}$ 7) $\frac{2}{25}$ 13) $7\frac{1}{2}$ 19) $\frac{1}{25}$ 25) $\frac{22}{25}$ 31) 2

3) $25\frac{1}{10}$ 9) $\frac{3}{10}$ 15) $\frac{13}{50}$ 21) $\frac{7}{1000}$ 27) $\frac{11}{50}$ 33) $\frac{7}{200}$

5) $\frac{77}{500}$ 11) $3\frac{7}{10}$ 17) $\frac{4}{25}$ 23) $\frac{21}{50}$ 29) $\frac{1}{40}$ 35) 19

Fractions to Decimals

1) .8	5) 4.3	9) 3.2	13) 1.5	17) .8571
3) .1	7) $\overline{.7}$	11) .875	15) .95	19) 115 hr; .1

Percents to Fractions

1) $\frac{1}{2}$	7) $\frac{2}{25}$	13) $\frac{7}{50}$	19) $\frac{107}{400}$	25) $\frac{3}{25}$	31) $\frac{17}{20}$; 17
3) $\frac{23}{200}$	9) $1\frac{4}{25}$	15) $\frac{13}{20}$	21) $\frac{3}{50}$	27) $\frac{1}{400}$	33) 3
5) $\frac{1}{25}$	11) $\frac{17}{40}$	17) $\frac{13}{25}$	23) $\frac{29}{400}$	29) $\frac{19}{50}$	35) $\frac{7}{200}$

Fractions to Percents

1) 57.14%	5) 11.11%	9) 25%	13) 12.5%	17) 71.11%; 28.89%
3) 50%	7) 180%	11) 175%	15) 92.86%	19) 33.33%

Percent-Base

1) 9	5) 40%	9) 150	13) 25%	17) 47%
3) 8	7) 9.6	11) 35%	15) 252	19) 121

Mixed Operations

1) .75; 75%	5) $\frac{33}{200}$; .165	9) $3\frac{3}{25}$; 3.12	13) 4.05; 405%	17) .3125; 31.25%
3) $\frac{21}{400}$; .0525	7) .06; 6%	11) $4\frac{1}{2}$; 450%	15) $\frac{1}{2500}$; .0004	19) $\frac{3}{500}$; .6%

Chapter 6 Problems

Ratios

1) $\frac{1}{3}$; .3333	5) $\frac{1}{3}$; .3333	9) $\frac{7}{10}$; .7	13) 77:100; $\frac{77}{100}$; 77 ÷ 100
3) $\frac{2}{5}$; .4	7) $\frac{3}{4}$; .75	11) 23:50; $\frac{23}{50}$; 23 ÷ 50	15) 27:20; $\frac{27}{20}$; 27 ÷ 20

Proportions

1) yes	5) no	9) yes	13) yes	17) yes
3) yes	7) no	11) no	15) yes	19) no

Solving Proportions

1) x = 15	7) x = 20	11) x = 2	15) x = 15	19) x = 12	23) 32 oz
3) x = 9	9) x = 2.45	13) x = 4	17) x = 1	21) $2\frac{2}{3}$ oz	25) 56 oz
5) x = 8					

Chapter 7 Problems

Volume Measurement

1) 12	5) 3	9) 2	13) $\frac{1}{8}$	17) 6
3) 2	7) $\frac{1}{2}$	11) 4	15) 16	19) 2

Length Measurement

1) 5280	5) 30	9) 12	13) 63360	17) 74
3) 4	7) $5\frac{1}{2}$	11) $\frac{1}{2}$	15) 96	19) 24

Mass Measurement

1) 48	5) 67.2	9) 62	13) 71	17) 83
3) 38	7) 7.5	11) 16	15) 11	19) 9.5

Reading a Ruler

See teacher's key for this section

Chapter 8 Problems

Prefixes and Abbreviations

1) kg, dl, dkm, l, mm, cg, hl, mg, g, dkl
3) kg, hl, dm, ml, g, dkm, cl, km, dkg, l

Volume Measurement

1) 2900	5) 14.2	9) 294.7	13) .00026	17) 100
3) 374.23	7) 60	11) 9.326	15) 8116	19) 2000

Length Measurement

1) 18760	5) 29000	9) 43000	13) 7.676	17) 6.921
3) 4.25	7) .00498	11) 1438.2	15) 11.19	19) 1.75

Mass Measurement

1) 8630	5) 436000000	9) 86300	13) .5611	17) 4650
3) 4.25	7) .4231	11) .0091164	15) 534000	19) 4000

Metric/English Conversions

1) 20, 90, 360, 195, 1125, 15, 960, 150	5) 2.724, 68.1, .448, .112	9) 720 cc
3) 5.46, .5, .62, .15	7) 58.6 kg	11) 1.3 pt

Chapter 9 Problems

1) 135	3) 90	5) 165	7) 60	9) 120

See teacher's key for angle drawing

Chapter 10 Problems

Making Change

1) give $ 1.00, say $30
   give $10.00, say $40
3) give $ .05, say $ 7
   give $ 1.00, say $ 8
   give $ 1.00, say $ 9
   give $ 1.00, say $10
5) give $ .01, say $2.89
   give $ .01, say $2.90
   give $ .10, say $3.00
   give $ 1.00, say $4.00
   give $ 1.00, say $5.00
   give $ 5.00, say $10.00

7) give $ .25, say $87.00
   give $ 1.00, say $88.00
   give $ 1.00, say $89.00
   give $ 1.00, say $90.00
   give $10.00, say $100.00
9) give $ 1.00, say $40.00
11) .10, .10, .25, .25, .25, 1, 1, 1
13) .01, .05, .10, .25, .25, .25, 1, 1
15) .10, .10, 1, 10, 20
17) 1, 10
19) .05, 1, 5

Receipts

See teacher's key for receipt writing

Balancing a Cash Drawer

1)

NUMBER	DENOMINATION	AMOUNT
37	PENNIES	.37
16	NICKELS	.80
30	DIMES	3.00
19	QUARTERS	4.75
	HALF DOLLARS	
41	$1 BILLS	41.00
7	$5 BILLS	35.00
5	$10 BILLS	50.00
6	$20 BILLS	120.00
5	CHECKS	147.89
	CASH IN DRAWER	402.81
	PLUS CASH PAID OUT	4.25
	TOTAL CASH	407.06
	LESS CHANGE	40.00
	CASH RECEIVED, CASHIER'S COUNT	367.06
	CASH RECEIVED, LEDGER COUNT	376.06
	AMOUNT OF CASH SHORT OR OVER	9.00 short

3)

NUMBER	DENOMINATION	AMOUNT
20	PENNIES	.20
17	NICKELS	1.05
12	DIMES	1.20
19	QUARTERS	4.75
	HALF DOLLARS	
27	$1 BILLS	27.00
16	$5 BILLS	80.00
14	$10 BILLS	140.00
7	$20 BILLS	140.00
6	CHECKS	210.00
	CASH IN DRAWER	604.20
	PLUS CASH PAID OUT	1.30
	TOTAL CASH	605.50
	LESS CHANGE	40.00
	CASH RECEIVED, CASHIER'S COUNT	565.50
	CASH RECEIVED, LEDGER COUNT	570.30
	AMOUNT OF CASH SHORT OR OVER	4.80 short

5)

NUMBER	DENOMINATION	AMOUNT
9	PENNIES	.09
12	NICKELS	.60
11	DIMES	1.10
17	QUARTERS	4.25
	HALF DOLLARS	
25	$1 BILLS	25.00
10	$5 BILLS	50.00
11	$10 BILLS	110.00
7	$20 BILLS	140.00
4	CHECKS	110.50
	CASH IN DRAWER	441.54
	PLUS CASH PAID OUT	6.00
	TOTAL CASH	447.54
	LESS CHANGE	35.00
	CASH RECEIVED, CASHIER'S COUNT	412.54
	CASH RECEIVED, LEDGER COUNT	302.04
	AMOUNT OF CASH SHORT OR OVER	110.50 over

Chapter 11 Problems

Elapsed Time

1) 5:57	5) 8:16	9) 6:27	13) 4:04; 4:00 = 8:04
3) 7:11	7) 5:19	11) 3:51; 3:56 = 7:47	15) 3:47; 3:37 = 7:24

Time Sheets

1) $7\frac{1}{2}$; $2\frac{1}{2}$; 15

	Theory	Demo	Practice
Scalp care	7	$3\frac{3}{4}$	14
Shampoo	$7\frac{3}{4}$	$3\frac{1}{4}$	15
Rinses	$4\frac{1}{2}$	$2\frac{3}{4}$	9
Water Manicure	11	4	$20\frac{1}{2}$
Oil Manicure	4	2	7
Hand/Arm Bleach	$1\frac{1}{2}$	$\frac{3}{4}$	2
Hand/Arm Massage	$1\frac{1}{2}$	$1\frac{1}{4}$	3
Hairstyling	$20\frac{1}{4}$	$9\frac{3}{4}$	$38\frac{3}{4}$
Cutting	$16\frac{1}{4}$	$8\frac{1}{2}$	34
Perm Waves	$22\frac{1}{2}$	$10\frac{3}{4}$	$43\frac{1}{4}$
Dyes,tints,etc	4	2	8
Facials	$7\frac{1}{4}$	3	16
Special masks	$6\frac{3}{4}$	3	15
Shop Management	10	5	10
Personality trn.	4	2	3
Gen. Business	6	$2\frac{1}{2}$	$5\frac{1}{4}$
Sanitation/Ster.	$16\frac{1}{4}$	8	20

3) $5\frac{3}{4}$; $\frac{3}{4}$; $6\frac{1}{2}$

	Theory	Demo	Practice
Scalp care	3	$1\frac{1}{4}$	1
Shampoo	$5\frac{1}{2}$	$2\frac{1}{2}$	$7\frac{1}{4}$
Rinses	$2\frac{1}{4}$	1	$1\frac{3}{4}$
Water Manicure	1	1	1
Hairstyling	$17\frac{1}{4}$	11	$15\frac{1}{2}$
Cutting	$15\frac{1}{2}$	14	18
Perm Waves	12	4	5
Facials	$9\frac{3}{4}$	$5\frac{1}{4}$	$10\frac{1}{2}$
Special masks	1	$\frac{1}{2}$	1
Shop Management	$5\frac{1}{2}$	$1\frac{1}{2}$	6
Anatomy/Phys.	1	0	0

5) $6\frac{1}{4}$; 3; $10\frac{3}{4}$

	Theory	Demo	Practice
Scalp care	10	$3\frac{1}{2}$	$15\frac{1}{4}$
Shampoo	10	$4\frac{3}{4}$	$12\frac{1}{4}$
Rinses	$7\frac{1}{2}$	$2\frac{1}{4}$	$10\frac{1}{2}$
Water Manicure	5	$4\frac{1}{2}$	$6\frac{3}{4}$
Oil Manicure	$1\frac{1}{2}$	1	$\frac{3}{4}$
Hand/Arm Massage	$\frac{3}{4}$	$\frac{3}{4}$	$1\frac{3}{4}$
Hairstyling	$25\frac{1}{4}$	$7\frac{1}{2}$	$41\frac{3}{4}$
Cutting	$30\frac{1}{2}$	$6\frac{1}{4}$	$31\frac{1}{4}$
Perm Waves	$17\frac{1}{2}$	$7\frac{1}{4}$	42
Dyes,tints,etc	$14\frac{3}{4}$	5	10
Facials	$6\frac{1}{2}$	4	10
Special masks	1	1	$3\frac{1}{2}$
Eyebrow Arching	3	1	1
Shop Management	4	2	$1\frac{1}{2}$
Personality trn.	$5\frac{1}{4}$	1	1
Gen. Business	$\frac{3}{4}$	1	$4\frac{1}{2}$
Sanitation/Ster.	$6\frac{3}{4}$	1	$7\frac{1}{2}$
Anatomy/Phys.	$18\frac{1}{2}$	1	3

Appointment Scheduling — times may vary

1) 8:00 perm, 9:30 perm, 10:15 updo, 11:00 shampoo/set, 8:00 hair cut, 9:30 hair cut, 11:45 frost, 12:00 frost

3) 8:00 bleach, 8:00 tint, 8:15 perm, 9:00 updo, 8:15 shampoo/set, 10:30 updo, 10:45 updo, 11:00 shampoo/set, 11:15 hair cut

5) 8:00 haircut, 8:15 haircut, 8:30 haircut, 8:30 perm, 9:15 bleach, 9:15 updo, 10:45 shampoo/set, 10:45 perm

---

Chapter 12 Problems

Gross Pay

1) $424.20	7) $386.38	11) $219.84	15) $557.70	19) $587.52	23) $3,041.33
3) $219.60	9) $494.30	13) $305.78	17) $352.00	21) $287.98	25) $183.75
5) $307.20					

Federal Income Tax

1) $16.03	5) $40.74	9) $39.24	13) $24.02; $24.75
3) $30.59	7) $27.27	11) $21.21	15) $45.99

State Income Tax

1) $ 47.50	5) $724.63	9) $395.40	13)	$461.67; $19.24
3) $416.81	7) $416.00	11) $29,172; $347.58	15)	$13,390.68; $334.22; $6.43

FICA Tax

1) $79.61	5) $31.47	9) $91.17	13) $16.44
3) $91.25	7) $158.99	11) $46.18	15) $50.92

Voluntary Deductions

1) $3.62; $2.48; $3.38; $3.53; $78.01   7) $36.95
3) $17.48; $10.82; $39.58; $46.04; $113.92   9) $4.04; $1.86; $2.86; $4.07; $77.83
5) $7.31; $3.69; $1.73; $22.73

Net Pay

1) $291.84; $27.68; $11.82; $21.92; $61.42; $230.42
3) $228.00; $10.98; $6156.00; $9.12; $17.12; $40.02; $187.98
5) $210.00; $25.04; $11.03; $15.77; $51.84; $158.16

Earning Statements

See teacher's key

Paychecks

See teacher's key

Chapter 13 Problems

Personal Checking

See teacher's key

Personal Savings

See teacher's key

Credit

Answers vary

Utility Bills

See teacher's key

Purchasing a Car

1) $9,494.64   3) $7,379.41   5) $14,870.58   7) $1346.91   9) $1696.24; $5,088.71

Budgeting

1) $1314.17; $420.53; $197.13; $197.13; $65.71; $65.71; $91.99; $65.71; $65.71; $78.85; and $65.71
3) $2360.00; $755.20; $354; $354; $118; $118; $165.20; $118; $118; $141.60; and $118
5) $5178; $1656.96; $776.70; $776.70; $258.90; $258.90; $362.46; $258.90; $258.90; $310.68; and $258.90
7) $1950.33; $624.11; $292.55; $292.55; $97.52; $97.52; $136.52; $97.52; $97.52; $117.02; and $97.52
9) $792; $253.44; $118.80; $118.80; $39.60; $39.60; $55.44; $ 39.60; $39.60; $47.52; and $39.60

Chapter 14 Problems

Commercial Discounts

Answers vary

Trade Discounts

1) $2.99; $11.96
3) $6.91; $79.42
5) $34.83; $64.68
7) $3.22; $39.66
9) $7.55; $30.20
11) $ 8.76; $166.35

13) $27.29; $232.66
15) $15.00; $85.00
17) $38.60; $214.50
19) $93.71; $281.12
21) $79.84; $74.85; $39.40; $99.75; $74.75 = $368.59
    Discount - $92.15; Net total - $276.44

Complement Discounts

1) 55%	7) 82%	13) .92; $79.42	19) .80; $30.20	25) .85; $85.00
3) 50%	9) 65%	15) .65; $64.68	21) .95; $166.35	27) .8475; $214.50
5) 80%	11) .80; $11.96	17) .925; $39.66	23) .895; $232.66	29) .75; $281.12

Series Discounts

1) $132.38; $397.13; $19.86; $377.27
3) $6.79; $61.09; $3.05; $58.04
5) $85.92; $773.23; $54.13; $719.10; $35.96; $683.14
7) $138.56; $785.15; $78.52; $706.63; $35.33; $671.30
9) $276.07; $1104.30; $110.43; $993.87; $49.69; $944.18
11) $13.43; $154.40; $7.72; $146.68; $2.93; $143.75
13) $177.34; $1596.01; $31.92; $1564.09
15) $45.48; $181.90; $18.19; $163.71; $11.46; $152.25

Single Equivalent Discount

1) .82935	7) .855	13) .55575	19) .783275	25) .468; $1697.87
3) .7938	9) .4704	15) .54	21) .72675; $114.79	
5) .605625	11) .57	17) .8096	23) .55575; $373.68	

Cash Discounts

1) June 28   3) January 28   5) November 30   7) $5.95; $291.42   9) $10.36; $507.46

Chapter 15 Problems

Sales Tax

1) $.78; $17.15   7) $.60; $10.59   13) $5.29; $105.96   17) $13,284.27; $11,195.60; $475.81
3) $.24; $7.19   9) $.30; $11.33   15) $.42; $9.75   19) $26.08
5) $1.48; $30.98 11) $.10; $1.98

Business Loans

1) .175	5) .1288	9) .1667	13) .5333	17) .2222
3) 5	7) .3472	11) .3333	15) 1.5	19) .75

Business Loans (continued)

1) $20.83; $1020.83
3) $70.83; $2620.83
5) $164; $2214

7) $67.46; $2467.46
9) $43.98; $1433.98
11) $233.33; $2233.33

13) $607.50; $4657.50
15) $1316.25; $7316.25

Business Loans (continued)

1) $45; $63.46; $2936.54
3) $90; $225.68; $7774.32
5) $84.89; $230.79; $7315.31